# The Antichrist

# THE ANTICHRIST

HILTON SUTTON, TH.D.

HSM PUBLICATIONS
ROMAN FOREST, TX

THE
ANTICHRIST



Hilton Sutton World Ministries
P.O. Box 1259
New Caney, Texas 77357

Cover Design: Kristin Miller



ISBN Number: 1-879503-21-2



Printed in the United States of America.

# Contents

# Foreword

By Kenneth Copeland

You and I are living in what the scriptures call the fullness of time. Our grandparents and those before them were only looking into this day. We're living in it. That's what makes it so important to have exact information about these times instead of ideas and speculations. This is especially true when we remember that theologians are not the only ones who have speculated on the Antichrist. Satan has seen to it that his crowd has come up with every kind of wild story you can think of, all of which are total lies.

Movie after movie has been made infecting the public with pure junk. This book you are about to read will arm you with chapter and verse concerning everything Satan is doing and planning to do. When people talk about the Antichrist taking over the world, you can boldly assure them that is not going to happen.

Only Adam was given the anointing to rule the world. He lost that anointing. Every person who has tried since has failed miserably. So will the Antichrist. Jesus, the last Adam, is the only one who will be successful in establishing a one-world government. Satan is defeated. So, anyone he "anoints" to do his work is defeated.

Another thing so helpful about *The Antichrist* is having a simple reference to the divine chronological order of coming events. Some people are looking for certain things to happen out of place. That causes confusion and breeds fear. We, as believers, are living in the love of God, not the wrath of God. Love, who is God, casts out fear. The eighth chapter deals with victory instead of fear. The Body of Christ has been delivered from fear. As I have said for years, "Read the back of the book. We win!" Dr. Sutton has given us a powerful tool to help us do that.

I now sum up this foreword by quoting Dr. Sutton in paragraph 4. "Stop allowing the devil to deceive and mislead you. Some Christians see the mark of the beast in many things and just know the Antichrist is right outside. Do not be gullible. Be Word-taught and correctly informed."

I have made a quality decision based on that admonition. I refuse to be misled, and I receive by faith the truth of God's Word about the days we are living in and those things that are ahead.

Rejoice! The Glory is here. We have a job to do and we will, with the Word, the Name and the Blood of Jesus, get it done.

JESUS IS LORD!

Kenneth Copeland

*"The coming of the lawless one*

*is according to the working of Satan,*

*with all power, signs, and lying wonders,"*

*—II Thessalonians 2:9 NKJ*

# The Antichrist

# Introduction

Nothing has created more of a stir of discussion in recent times than the discussion of the future events, and in particular, the Antichrist.

It was my good fortune to practically be raised in the church. Both my grandfather and father were ministers. When I was seven, I first heard the term "Antichrist." Then I began to hear more and more things said about him. I later was to learn that much of what was said was not always Biblically sound. But it was the opinion and the ideas of theologians of their time; and the generation before them. From a very careful study of the Word of God, we can learn the absolute truth about the Antichrist; and never again be caught up in speculation or in fear.

With the help and authority of the scriptures, not someone's theology or the speculation of so-called experts, we want to discover the exact Biblical identity and characteristics of the Antichrist.

Therefore, we must avoid individual doctrines, individual views or individual "revelations from God." We must depend upon exactly what the Word of God says about this important subject matter.

The subject of this book is the Antichrist. There is much information concerning the one who becomes the Antichrist. We will focus on him directly from the scripture.

This has been a major subject within the church for many years and, quite often, misunderstood.

Drawing information only from God's Word, one has an accurate picture of the Antichrist. Understanding his satanic assignment and the time allotted to him becomes clear. One learns he utterly fails to carry out his evil assignment.

Please read every word very carefully and then go back through this book again and again until this material becomes yours. Your friends and family will be amazed at your knowledge when you share these truths.

Reading carefully, you will discover many of your questions about the Antichrist are going to be answered. Also, some things you may have been taught by well-meaning people were not Biblically correct. You will discover how to correct them by the use of God's Word, the Bible.

## INTRODUCTION

Let's begin with a statement of our Lord Jesus in Matthew 24:4, ***"…Take heed that no one deceives you."*** The Apostle Paul also addresses deception in II Thessalonians 2:3 *NKJ* where he writes, ***"Let no one deceive you by any means…"*** This is a more detailed statement than the one made by Jesus in Matthew 24. Take a close look at Paul's statement because he is dealing with the revealing of the Antichrist. His statement is in perfect harmony with that of Jesus; guarding oneself against being deceived. The Holy Scriptures, if studied and accepted, serve to inoculate one against deception.

***"Let no one deceive you by any means"***—not by their personality, their oratorical ability, their use of scripture taken out of context, or their ability to perform what appears to be signs and wonders. Paul points out that the works of the Antichrist and the False Prophet are lying miracles, lying wonders; therefore, they are designed to be extremely deceptive.

> ***"The coming of the lawless one is according to the working of Satan, with all power, signs, and lying wonders,"***
>
> —II Thessalonians 2:9 *NKJ*

Jesus goes on to say in Matthew 24:5, ***"For many will come in My name, saying, 'I am the Christ…'"*** We know the word "Christ" interpreted from the Greek means the ***"anointed one,"*** so Jesus is saying, ***"There will come those who will declare themselves to be the anointed one."*** When we study all of the Biblical references concerning the Antichrist, we learn that at mid-tribulation, from the city of Jerusalem, the Antichrist will declare himself to be God, the ***"anointed one."*** **(II Thessalonians 2:4)**

Jesus continues, ***"For many will come in My name, saying, 'I am the Christ,' and will deceive many."*** We have had examples of this down through the ages and even to this very day. Sometimes even Christians are deceived and misled because of their failure to know the scriptures. With a lack of knowledge of God's Word, one is easy prey for an imposter, or a religious con man, particularly one who comes with so-called spiritual overtures.

The words of Jesus are quite direct, and the words of Paul certainly add great authority.

All of the information in the Word of God concerning the Antichrist must be important or it would not be there. Once in a while I hear someone comment about information in the

Bible, concerning the Book of Revelation and the Antichrist, ***"Well I just don't need to understand that. It is not important to me."***

Please understand this: If it is in the Book, it is important to you, whether you think so or not! Were it not so, God would not have put it in His Book. There is nothing between its covers that is insignificant. Everything in this Book is of vital importance to us. Do not "cop out" on any part of God's Word. Study so that "copping out" is never necessary.

Theologians and Bible teachers of today have a distinct advantage over their predecessors. We now live in the conclusion of the Last Days. The ancient prophecies of the Scriptures are now being fulfilled and with pinpoint accuracy.

The Apostle Peter records a profound truth which governs the interpretation of the prophecies of the Holy Scripture.

> "For we have not followed cunningly devised fables, when we made known unto you the power and coming of our Lord Jesus Christ, but were eyewitnesses of his majesty. For he received from God the Father honour and glory, when there came such a voice to him from the excellent glory, This is my beloved Son,

> in whom I am well pleased. And this voice which came from heaven we heard, when we were with him in the holy mount.
>
> We have also a more sure word of prophecy; whereunto ye do well that ye take heed, as unto a light that shineth in a dark place, until the day dawn, and the day star arise in your hearts: Knowing this first, that no prophecy of the scripture is of any private interpretation. For the prophecy came not in old time by the will of man: but holy men of God spake as they were moved by the Holy Ghost."
>
> —II Peter 1:16–21

The Scripture is absolute; Bible prophecies are not left up to personal interpretation. You, nor I, have any right to our own opinions about what God has stated. However, we do have the right to believe, with simple God-given faith, exactly what the Scriptures declare.

Since Isaiah 35:8 declares, "The wayfaring men will not err therein"; He strongly implies, God has stated exactly what He wanted to say and mankind should not struggle over its meaning.

# Biblical Identification of the Antichrist

*"Can the Antichrist*

*be Biblically identified?"*

CHAPTER ONE

# Biblical Identification of the Antichrist

People, young and old, from every walk of life, want to know exactly WHO is going to be the Antichrist. A major question arises. Can we personally identify the Antichrist? The answer to that, based on the authority of the scripture, is "**NO.**" There is not a person alive who knows the identity of the Antichrist. This statement might shock you, because we have heard many "predictions" from so many learned scholars as to whom he might be!

Those who attempt to name such a person are speculating and have no Biblical support. This point allows me to make the following statement:

**Speculation is always based on ignorance of the subject under discussion!**

There have been a number of people, from time to time, who have been nominated to be the Antichrist. The only problem is that those people pass from the scene and, of course, once a person dies they are appointed unto judgment. They will not come back and become the Antichrist.

Recently a popular opinion, within the ranks of some prophetic teachers, was that King Juan Carlos of Spain is the Antichrist. Not so. You will discover as we study the scriptures that he certainly does not fit the description of Antichrist in the Holy Bible. Isn't it strange. Henry Kissinger once had this dubious nomination. Some have even suggested Prince Charles of England and Bill Gates of Microsoft. Utterly ridiculous! None of these men fit the Biblical description of the Antichrist.

It is not Biblically possible for anyone to personally identify the Antichrist, and those who attempt to do so are, without exception, speculating. Therefore, when people get off the main track on the subject of the Antichrist, don't go along with them. Do not listen to what they have to say, as you are likely to become confused and misled.

Now I ask a similar question, ***"Can the Antichrist be identified?"*** Notice I have left out the word "personally." I said "No" to the first question, but the next question is, ***"Can the Antichrist be Biblically identified?"*** The answer to that question is **"YES."**

Follow me very carefully as I am going to provide you a list of scriptures. In Daniel 7:8 the Antichrist is called the ***"little horn."*** In Daniel 8:23, he is referred to as a ***"king,"*** denoting that he is a strong diplomat or national leader.

The Apostle Paul in 2 Thessalonians 2:3, refers to him as the ***"man of sin"*** and the ***"son of perdition."*** The word ***"perdition"*** means ***"destruction."*** Then in 2 Thessalonians 2:8, he is referred to as the ***"lawless one"*** or ***"wicked one."*** In 1 John 2:18, John simply identifies him as the ***"Antichrist,"*** the term most used to identify him.

So we have Biblical terms of identification: the ***"little horn," "king," "man of sin," "son of destruction (perdition)," "lawless one,"*** and the ***"Antichrist."*** All of those terms from both Old and New Testaments identify the person who is destined to become the Antichrist.

We know from the information that within the scripture the Antichrist is a human being; and he is a man. Thank God women are not considered for this assignment. We learn much about the Antichrist from the Book of Daniel in the Old Testament and the writings of the Apostles Paul and John in the New Testament. They give more insight to the exact identity of the Antichrist than any other references within the scripture.

There are scriptures pertaining to the Antichrist in the Book of Revelation, but oftentimes they are repetitions of what we have already discovered within the writings of the prophet Daniel. However, Revelation spells out his evil assignment and utter defeat.

### The Little Horn

> *"After this I saw in the night visions, and behold a fourth beast, dreadful and terrible, and strong exceedingly; and it had great iron teeth: it devoured and brake in pieces, and stamped the residue with the feet of it: and it was diverse from all the beasts that were before it; and it had ten horns. I considered the horns, and, behold, there came up among them another little horn, before whom there were three of the first horns plucked up by*

*the roots: and, behold, in this horn were eyes like the eyes of man, and a mouth speaking great things."*

—Daniel 7:7–8

*"Then I heard one saint speaking, and another saint said unto that certain saint which spake, How long shall be the vision concerning the daily sacrifice, and the transgression of desolation, to give both the sanctuary and the host to be trodden under foot?"*

—Daniel 8:13

We find the Antichrist in the seventh chapter of the Book of Daniel identified a "little horn." The reason he is called the little horn is because he rises among a group of ten horns. These ten horns are nations. They are clarified for us by the Prophet Daniel and the 17th chapter of the Book of Revelation. We know that the ten horns prophesied by Daniel, referred to by John, in the Book of Revelation, identify the Common Market of Europe. The current membership in the

European Economic Community involves more than enough for the ten nations that are described in the Book of Daniel.

We know that the western division of the former Roman Empire is identified by this description.

The Roman Empire had two major divisions—western and eastern. It was made up by ten sub-divisions, accounting for the ten horns. The ten horns in Revelation 17 also identify the ten major European nations that will be the support for the Antichrist. John the Revelator states that this beast was different from all that were before it and it had ten horns.

The system of European nations that provide the Antichrist a base of operations is called a Beast in the Book of Revelation. All the Beast before it are the empires of Egypt, Assyria, Babylon, Persia, Greece and Rome.

The Roman Empire is identified by the legs of iron and feet of iron and clay in Daniel Chapter Two. The ten toes of the image of Daniel 2 correspond to the ten horns of both Daniel and Revelation.

One may ask, "Why are the ten nations which support the Antichrist identified only with the western division of the Roman Empire?"

The answer lies in that the eastern division is, for the most part, Arab or Muslim. When studying the books of Isaiah and

Zechariah one discovers the Arab nations do not accept or support the Antichrist. Also note that it wasn't until 293 A.D., over two hundred-twenty years after the Romans destroyed Jerusalem in 68–70 A.D., that the Empire first had two divisions.

As the little horn, he rises among ten nations that support him. It becomes evident, as we research additional scripture concerning him, that he has opposition in due course of time, from three of the major nations that enabled him to rise to power. He, being a capable diplomat, has the power from the other nations, to put down the opposition. Please notice the terminology used to describe these three horns (or nations) that rebelled against him; they were "plucked out by the roots."

Some translations would indicate that he just suppresses them. But when I look at this term and run its Hebrew references, it appears that he absolutely defeats them and gains total control over them. They no longer have authority of their own.

So we know him to be the little horn that rises among the ten major nations that provide his base of operation in Europe.

## KING

> ***"And the ten horns out of this kingdom are ten kings that shall arise: and another shall rise after them; and***

> *he shall be diverse from the first, and he shall subdue three kings."*
>
> —Daniel 7:24

In Daniel 7:24 he is spoken of as a king. One might eventually consider him as the president of the European Economic Community. He will be the man who will lead that community during the seven years of Tribulation.

## MAN OF SIN—SON OF PERDITION

> *"Let no man deceive you by any means: for that day shall not come, except there come a falling away first, and that man of sin be revealed, the son of perdition;"*
>
> —II Thessalonians 2:3

The Apostle Paul refers to the Antichrist as the "man of sin." From this reference, we add another facet to the identity of the Antichrist, "the son of perdition." As the man of sin, we realized his plan to be totally evil.

The dictionary gives the definition of the word "perdition" as "destruction." Destruction, failure without victory and a loss of everything await him. We should have picked up on that long ago from the pen of Paul.

### LAWLESS ONE—THE WICKED ONE

> ***"And then shall that Wicked be revealed, whom the Lord shall consume with the spirit of his mouth, and shall destroy with the brightness of his coming."***
>
> —II Thessalonians 2:8

### FALSE PRETENDER

There is yet one more Biblical identity of this man. It is found in the writings of John.

> ***"Little children, it is the last time: and as ye have heard that antichrist shall come, even now are there many antichrists; whereby we know that it is the last time."***
>
> —1 John 2:18

Why would they have heard? The answer is found in the writings of the Apostle Paul. However, it is from John that we get the term Antichrist. From Jesus comes the term "false Christ." False Christ includes all who have come or may come declaring themselves to be "THE" anointed one.

The Word of God reveals his full identity. He is the little horn that rises among the ten major nations that have created the European Economic Community. Rising to be the leader of that amalgamation of European nations; therefore he is referred to as a "king." He is a man of sin. Nothing about him is of God.

Please understand he is not God's agent. He is not God's servant. God is not doing anything through him or using him. He is called the son of perdition. Paul reveals that Jesus is going to destroy him. One knows what his end is going to be, before even getting into the details of the Book of Revelation.

We discover that he is the wicked one or the lawless one. He will deny that Jesus is the Christ, thus denying the Father also (1 John 2:22), and that Jesus came in the flesh (1 John 4:3, II John 7). We sum up all of this together with the term that is most commonly used, "the Antichrist."

Daniel 9:24–27 provides even more insight to the Antichrist.

> ***"Seventy weeks are determined upon thy people and upon thy holy city, to finish the transgression, and to***

> *make an end of sins, and to make reconciliation for iniquity, and to bring in everlasting righteousness, and to seal up the vision and prophecy, and to anoint the most Holy. Know therefore and understand, that from the going forth of the commandment to restore and to build Jerusalem unto the Messiah the Prince shall be seven weeks, and threescore and two weeks: the street shall be built again, and the wall, even in troublous times. And after threescore and two weeks shall Messiah be cut off, but not for himself: and the people of the prince that shall come shall destroy the city and the sanctuary; and the end thereof shall be with a flood, and unto the end of the war desolations are determined. And he shall confirm the covenant with many for one week: and in the midst of the week he shall cause the sacrifice and the oblation to cease, and for the overspreading of abominations he shall make it desolate, even until the consummation, and that determined shall be poured upon the desolate."*
>
> —Daniel 9:24–27

God is speaking to Daniel about his people and the city of Jerusalem. These seventy weeks are weeks of years, not weeks of days, creating a total of 490 years. There are six things that must be accomplished for Daniel's people, the Jewish race, and the Holy City, Jerusalem.

1. To finish the transgression.
2. To make an end of sins.
3. To make reconciliation for iniquity.
4. To bring in everlasting righteousness.
5. To seal up the vision and the prophecy.
6. To anoint the most holy.

We know that these six major items that God must bring about for the people of Israel and the City of Jerusalem have not yet been accomplished.

During the Persian Empire, the Persian kings permitted Ezra, Zerubbabel and Nehemiah to take more than 50,000 Israeli captives out of Persia and return to Jerusalem. This company rebuilt the city of Jerusalem and a second temple. The Book of Nehemiah reveals it was in very troublesome times. The rebuilding took seven weeks or 49 years.

Then another 62 weeks transpires and the Messiah shall be cut off, but not for Himself. This is in the reference to the crucifixion of the Lord Jesus Christ after a full 69 weeks. He was crucified outside the city of Jerusalem, just as the scripture prophesies. Only one week of Daniel's prophecy remains unfulfilled, the 70th.

History records that the city of Jerusalem and the second Temple were destroyed by the Romans in 70 A.D. as an exact prophecy of the Lord Jesus Christ found in Matthew 24, Mark 13, and Luke 21.

As we look closely at Daniel 9:24–27, we find that he, referring to the other prince (The Antichrist), shall confirm a covenant (an agreement or a treaty) with many for one week. However, in the middle of the last seven-year period of God's revelation to Daniel the Antichrist breaks the agreement. He makes it impossible for any religious activity to continue in Jerusalem.

We know this about our adversary, the devil. He, of himself, can do nothing. He must always have a human instrument through which to work; someone whom he has so completely deceived, that they permit him to possess them. Therefore, he has their talents, their ability, and their resources all available to him. He then, through that person, attempts to do what otherwise he could not do.

So he that caused the destruction of Jerusalem and the Second Temple in 70 A.D. was none other than Satan; and he was using the Roman legions to put down a Jewish rebellion.

Again it is Satan who will use the Antichrist to confirm a covenant, or work out a treaty, with the nation of Israel for seven years. But in the middle of that seven-year period, he will break that treaty and turn on Israel.

# A MAN WHO HEADS AN ORGANIZATION

*"But in his estate shall he honour the God of forces:*

*and a god whom his fathers knew not shall he*

*honour with gold, and silver, and with*

*precious stones, and pleasant things."*

*—Daniel 11:38*

Chapter Two

# A Man Who Heads an Organization

Again, we refer to Daniel 9:24–27 for additional insight about the Antichrist.

What does this passage of scripture add to the identity of the Antichrist?

## Diplomat

He is a diplomat of the first order. He is well-versed in government. Since he rises among the powers of Europe to the position of the leader of the European Federation, he would have to be a diplomat of the very highest order. He has the authority, due to his position of leadership in Europe, to enter into an agreement with Israel for seven years. That seven-year period is the 70th week of the prophecy set forth by our Heavenly Father in Daniel 9.

The seventieth week of Daniel 9 is also the same as the seven-year period we know as the Tribulation.

## World Class Economist

He is also a world-class economist. To lead and bring Europe into a very prominent position, he would not only have to be a very shrewd diplomat and governmental leader, but also one who is an economic genius as well. We know that Europe becomes a very prosperous entity prior to the Tribulation. We are hearing voices that state Europe must rise to become the most prominent entity on the earth; and the United States must fade away. The Word of God does not support the demise of the United States. Please reference my material covering "The United States in Prophecy."

However, Europe will continue to gain in strength and prominence. It is out of that area that the Antichrist will arise.

## Military Strategist

We also know from the 11th chapter of the Book of Daniel the Antichrist to be a very capable military strategist.

You would have to search long to find his equal. He has much military opposition during the Tribulation period. So it is necessary that he be an outstanding military strategist. Daniel 8:24b declares, "He will destroy wonderfully."

> ***"But in his estate shall he honour the God of forces: and a god whom his fathers knew not shall he honour with gold, and silver, and with precious stones, and pleasant things."***
>
> —Daniel 11:38

As I was growing up, the theology of that day, and for many yet today, was that he would be Jewish and from Assyria. The theological reasoning was, he would have to be Jewish or Israel would never enter into a seven-year treaty with him. This is not so, in that Israel at this present time is an associate member of the Common Market of Europe.

Requiring him to be an Assyrian does not hold up either. It is believed by many that since the man who was the first type of Antichrist, was the great Assyrian general, Antiochus Epiphanes, the Antichrist would therefore be from Assyria. Epiphanes was attempting to conquer Judah. Judah was the southern half of Israel, after the death of Solomon, made up of the tribes of Judah and Benjamin.

Judah eventually represented all the tribes because of the migration from the ten tribes of the north to Judah. The ten tribes of the north fell into immediate idolatry and rebellion against the God of Abraham, Isaac and Jacob. The devout one's made their way south to become part of Judah so that in due course of time Judah represented all of the 12 tribes. You will find this fact in the books of First and Second Chronicles, as well as Ezekiel 36 and 37.

To declare the Antichrist has to be an Assyrian because the first type of the Antichrist was an Assyrian is stretching the point. We do not know from Biblical record what his exact nationality is going to be.

It is simply theological speculation that he will be Jewish and an Assyrian. Daniel 11:37 states, "He will regard not the God of his fathers." However, this verse does not necessarily establish his religion. There has been enough guesswork on the subject of the Antichrist. It is now time for us to allow the Holy Scriptures to speak for themselves. Personal opinions can not replace Biblical chapter and verse.

# HIS CHARACTER AND PERSONALITY

*"And his power shall be mighty, but not by his own power: and he shall destroy wonderfully, and shall prosper, and practice, and shall destroy the mighty and the holy people."*

*—Daniel 8:24*

Chapter Three

# His Character and Personality

Recall Daniel 7:8 that we read earlier; then go to verse 20. We begin to discover the character and personality of the Antichrist.

> *"I considered the horns, and, behold, there came up among them another little horn, before whom there were three of the first horns plucked up by the roots: and, behold, in this horn were eyes like the eyes of man, and a mouth speaking great things."*
>
> *—Daniel 7:8*

> *"And of the ten horns that were in his head, and of the other which came up, and before whom three fell; even of that horn that had eyes, and a mouth that*

*spake very great things, whose look was more stout than his fellows."*

*—Daniel 7:20*

In the Biblical references of Daniel 7:8 and Daniel 7:20 attention is drawn to his eyes. From these scriptures we learn he is a visionary and a spiritualist seer.

## A Visionary

We have visionaries today.

Napoleon, Charlemagne, and Alexander the Great were visionaries. We've had Godly visionaries like John G. Lake, Stanley Livingston, P.C. Nelson, Smith Wigglesworth, and others. We have visionaries among us today, such as Oral Roberts, T. L. Osborn, Dwight Moody, and Billy Graham. God fearing visionaries are spoken of by the prophet Joel in Chapter 2, verses 28–29.

Visionaries are men whose vision extended beyond the community in which their church is located. They envision their city, county, state, or nation and begin reaching out from their base of operation. They then launch their ministerial attack against the works of the Enemy, Satan.

The Antichrist, from the references in Daniel 7:8 and 7:20, is a visionary, however ungodly. He is satanically motivated to envision becoming king of the world.

### A Great Orator

We also learn from these same references that he speaks pompous words. He is quite an orator. Let's discover also in Daniel 7:11 and Daniel 7:25, his ability as an effective orator.

> *"I beheld then because of the voice of the great words which the horn spake: I beheld even till the beast was slain, and his body destroyed, and given to the burning flame."*
>
> *—Daniel 7:11*

> *"And he shall speak great words against the most High, and shall wear out the saints of the most High, and think to change times and laws: and they shall be given into his hand until a time and times and the dividing of time."*
>
> *—Daniel 7:25*

These are the references to his speaking pompous words. Daniel 7:25 is also in reference to his ability to attempt to sway people his way by a flood of words.

In verse 25 it states that he speaks pompous words against the most high. This causes us to understand that he does not mind speaking out against God. In due course of time, he is going to announce himself as God. I prefer to identify him as an "orator of orators," one who is capable of holding an audience spellbound by his oratory, as long as he would desire. Hitler and Mussolini both had this ability.

> ***"I beheld, and the same horn (THIS IS THE ANTICHRIST) made war with the saints, and prevailed against them;"***
>
> ***—Daniel 7:21***

## Persecutor

We learn yet additional information about his character and personality from the 7th chapter in the Book of Daniel. We discover that he is a persecutor.

> *"I beheld, and the same horn made war with the saints, and prevailed against them; And he shall speak great words against the most High, and shall wear out the saints of the most High, and think to change times and laws: and they shall be given into his hand until a time and times and the dividing of time."*
>
> *—Daniel 7:21, 25*

Time, times and half of time identifies the last three and one-half years of the Tribulation. Therefore, we know that the saints he makes war against, some of which he will overcome, are those who are accepting the Lord Jesus Christ during the second half of the Tribulation. According to Revelation 14:6–7, angels preach the Gospel to every nation in their own language during the last half of the Tribulation.

Isaiah 55:11 declares, ***"So shall my word be that goeth forth out of my mouth: it shall not return unto me void, but it shall accomplish that which I please, and it shall prosper in the thing whereto I sent it."***

There will be a host of people saved right under the nose of the Antichrist in the second half of the Tribulation. Against some of them he makes war. A number of them are martyred by him. Daniel 7:21, 25 reveal the Antichrist prevailing over some of the saints during the second half of the Tribulation. Revelation Chapter Five also speaks of martyrs in the same period of time. Not only is he a visionary and an orator, he is a persecutor.

### LAWYER

We also discover from verse 25 that he intends to change times and law. We learn from this that he is a lawyer.

> ***"And then shall that Wicked be revealed, whom the Lord shall consume with the spirit of his mouth, and shall destroy with the brightness of his coming: Even him, whose coming is after the working of Satan with all power and signs and lying wonders."***
>
> ***—II Thessalonians 2:8–9***

This above scripture refers to the Antichrist as the "lawless one." I don't want to cast a disparaging shadow over lawyers, but the Antichrist is going to be extremely well-versed in the law of his day; and will attempt to change the laws. Let me illustrate.

We now have lawyers in America that work for institutions, such as the ACLU. They are constantly working to change, revise and rewrite the American Constitution and the Bill of Rights. We cannot afford to allow them to do so. Those instruments were divinely created by the Almighty through our founding fathers. We must stand up and refuse to allow evil attorneys to constantly re-interpret our Constitution and thus, rewrite it to fit their agenda. So the Antichrist is going to be a lawyer, who wants everything to be the way he desires.

## Fierce Facial Features

The first half of Daniel 8:23 tells us that he has very fierce features, as well as a very strong, powerful countenance. You would not attempt to stare him down.

> *"And in the latter time of their kingdom, when the transgressors are come to the full, a king of fierce countenance, and understanding dark sentences, shall stand up."*
>
> *—Daniel 8:23*

## Spiritualist Medium

In the last part of Daniel 8:23 it states, ***"He understands sinister schemes."*** He is a spiritualist medium of the highest order. This man has quite a versatile character. He is literally possessed by Satan, who uses his talents, ability, knowledge, education, and resources as though they were his. Satan will prompt him to excel in every facet of his multiple character.

We have learned from Daniel 8:23, that he is a spiritualist medium who not only understands sinister schemes, but the language of the dark side of the Spirit world. Remember, the Apostle Paul teaches that he is going to be working signs and wonders. Paul states they are false, not real. 2 Thessalonians 2:9 refers to them as "lying signs and wonders." The Book of Revelation also makes reference to the signs and wonders. Likewise, the False Prophet is also working lying signs and wonders. This information certainly identifies spiritualist mediums attempting to deceive the people.

## Powerful, with Great Ability

> ***"And his power shall be mighty, but not by his own power: and he shall destroy wonderfully, and shall***

> *prosper, and practice, and shall destroy the mighty and the holy people."*
>
> *—Daniel 8:24*

He is a very powerful man, physically. He is a very powerful leader. Where does he get this authority? Notice verse 24 says, *"mighty...but not by his own power..."*

> *"And the beast which I saw was like unto a leopard, and his feet were as the feet of a bear, and his mouth as the mouth of a lion: and the dragon gave him his power, and his seat, and great authority. And they worshipped the dragon which gave power unto the beast: and they worshipped the beast, saying, Who is like unto the beast? who is able to make war with him?*
>
> *—Revelation 13:2,4*

Revelation 13:2, 4 identifies the source of his power. It is none other than the dragon clearly defined by the Book of Revelation to be that old serpent, the devil and Satan.

*"And when the dragon saw that he was cast unto the earth, he persecuted the woman which brought forth the man child."*

*—Revelations 12:13*

The dragon of Revelation 12:13 is also the serpent who was present in the Garden of Eden. It is from him that the Antichrist gets his authority and his power; and from no other source. Let me emphasize he is not God's agent. God is NOT using him.

### Deceitful

***"And through his policy also he shall cause craft to prosper in his hand; and he shall magnify himself in his heart, and by peace shall destroy many: he shall also stand up against the Prince of princes; but he shall be broken without hand."***

***—Daniel 8:25***

The Antichrist will be extremely deceitful. Jesus and the Apostle Paul admonish us to take heed that we are not deceived by any means. Through his cunning and deceit, his rule will prosper for a time, in one-fourth of the earth. Revelation 6:8 provides the area of his influence.

He has only seven years in which to try and succeed at Satan's plan. He has tremendous opposition. We will examine the opposition later in this book.

> ***"Even him, whose coming is after the working of Satan with all power and signs and lying wonders, And with all deceivableness of unrighteousness in them that perish; because they received not the love of the truth, that they might be saved."***
>
> ***— II Thessalonians 2:9–10***

The Apostle Paul provides insight into the Antichrist, as does Daniel and Revelation.

Here is another scripture that clearly identifies his source as Satan. The coming of the lawless one is according to the working of Satan with all power, signs, and lying wonders, and with all unrighteous deception among those who perish.

Why are they perishing? Some people choose to heed his voice and to follow him. They receive the mark of the beast and worship the image of the beast; and that seals their doom.

## He Uses Flattery

> ***"Now when they shall fall, they shall be aided with a little help: but many shall cleave to them with flatteries."***
>
> ***—Daniel 11:34***

We are discovering from Daniel 11:34, along with what we discovered in Daniel 8:25 and 2 Thessalonians 2:10, that not only is he cunning and very deceitful, but he will use flattery.

We've already read in Daniel 11:25 *NKJ*, ***"He shall stir up his power and his courage against the king of the south, with a great army. And the king of the south shall be stirred up to battle with a great and mighty army, but he shall not stand, for they shall devise plans against him."***

Look again at verse 34, "Now when they fall, they shall be aided with a little help, but many shall join them with intrigue." The word "intrigue" is "flattery." The cunning, deceitful ability of the Antichrist will also include his use of flattery.

Isn't it interesting that we are learning much from just the Word of God about the character and personality of the Antichrist?

## REGARDS NOT GOD OF HIS FATHERS

> *"Neither shall he regard the God of his fathers, nor the desire of women, nor regard any god: for he shall magnify himself above all."*
>
> *—Daniel 11:37*

This verse reveals he has a religious background or a godly background. His people, from which he originated, his nationality, knew God. He regards not the god of his fathers. This is the verse that some use to say that he has to be Jewish. There are many of us from different denominations who have generations in the ranks of our family that truly worshipped God. Why couldn't the backslidden son of a Gentile family that has long relationships with the God of Abraham, Isaac and Jacob be the Antichrist?

The Antichrist is not necessarily Jewish. There are vast numbers of Gentiles today that truly worship God and know the Lord Jesus Christ as their personal Savior. So why could he not come from that type of background? We have nothing in the Bible that says he won't, but we also have nothing in the Bible that says he will be Jewish.

## Homosexual

Not only does he not regard the religion and the God of his fathers, but this same verse of scripture in Daniel 11:37 says he will have no desire of women. This is of interest; He is homosexual. The Antichrist is a homosexual.

> ***"Neither shall he regard the God of his fathers,* <u>nor the desire of women</u>*, nor regard any god: for he shall magnify himself above all."***
>
> ***—Daniel 11:37***

One needs to have more than one reference in the scripture to absolutely solidify or put into concrete a Biblical truth.

Revelation 11:8, with the additional insight from Chapter 13 and II Thessalonians 2:4, makes clear the Antichrist moves his headquarters out of Europe and into Jerusalem at the middle of the Tribulation.

Once the Antichrist moves his headquarters and all of his company into Jerusalem, it becomes known as Sodom. Sodom! Jerusalem, where our Lord was crucified, would be known as Sodom! That is the exact statement in Revelation 11:8.

> *"And their dead bodies shall lie in the street of the great city, which spiritually is called Sodom and Egypt, where also our Lord was crucified."*
>
> *—Revelations 11:8*

This verse confirms Daniel 11:37 that he is homosexual. There is another reference in Daniel 7:20 where it speaks of his fellows, those that surround, support, work with and under him.

> *"And of the ten horns that were in his head, and of the other which came up, and before whom three fell; even of that horn that had eyes, and a mouth that spake very great things, whose look was more stout than his* **fellows.***"*
>
> *—Daniel 7:20*

When one researches the word "fellows," as it is used in Daniel 7:20, in the Hebrew, one discovers that it is the feminine use of the word. We have three distinct references in the scripture that clearly identify the Antichrist as being homosexual.

We've read many scriptures that identify the character and the personality of the Antichrist. We've learned that he is a visionary, an orator, a persecutor, and lawyer. He has a powerful countenance, and is a spiritualist medium of the first echelon. He is very powerful having Satan as his source, and is extremely deceitful using flattery. He regards not the god of his fathers, and has no desire of women.

***Let's review who the Antichrist is NOT:***

For sure, he is not any of the male personalities that have been selected by confused theologians.

We do not know his personal identity and there is nothing in the scripture that allows us to speculate concerning the personal identity of the Antichrist. No one on this earth knows who he is nor can his personal identity be revealed until after the Church and Old Testament righteous have been caught away from Earth to Heaven. Any name that anyone comes up with is pure speculation.

I have heard throughout my lifetime teaching that Judas would come back and be the Antichrist because he is spoken of as the Son of Perdition. That's only one of the terms that identifies the Antichrist and simply because that it is also used in identifying Judas does not establish that Judas will be resurrected and be the Antichrist.

The Antichrist is not Judas. Nor was he Hitler or Mussolini. Many preachers from evangelical, fundamentalist and Full Gospel backgrounds selected Hitler or Mussolini as the Antichrist from the mid-1930s to 1940s. Neither is he Franklin Delano Roosevelt. Though I heard back in the 1940s after the death of President Roosevelt in 1944 that because it was a closed coffin funeral there were those foolish Christians that said, "Aha, he's not there," and Roosevelt, who was such a man of great influence would be the Antichrist.

These fickle ones later jumped on the bandwagon for Henry Kissinger. They worked out a mathematical formula and when you added the numbers alongside the letters of Kissinger's name, it totaled 666.

Then they jumped from Henry Kissinger to King Juan Carlos of Spain. They moved from Juan Carlos to thinking that it's possibly Prince Charles of England. A couple of years ago an e-mail notified everyone that in reality Bill Gates of Microsoft was the Antichrist.

NONE of these men fit the biblical description of the Antichrist found within the pages of God's Word. They may have had one or two characteristics, but that's all.

Plain and simple, the Antichrist is not someone that we can identify today. Remember, he is not a religious leader as some have proposed in the past.

We have learned much about the Antichrist's characteristics and personality. Possessing the biblical description of the Antichrist, one is free from childlike games based only on speculation.

# His Assignment

*"And I looked, and behold a pale horse:*
*and his name that sat on him was Death,*
*and Hell followed with him. And power was*
*given unto them over the fourth part of the*
*earth, to kill with sword, and with hunger,*
*and with death, and with the*
*beasts of the earth."*

*—Revelation 6:8*

CHAPTER FOUR

# His Assignment

The Word of God provides us the assignment of the Antichrist, given him by Satan.

> ***"I beheld, and the same horn made war with the saints, and prevailed against them;"***
>
> ***—Daniel 7:21***

I was watching, and the same horn (which is the little horn that is spoken of as a king, the man of sin, the son of perdition, the wicked one, the Antichrist) was making war against the saints and prevailing against them.

Several references already covered cause us to know he prevails over some of the saints of the second half of the Tribulation. Notice once again he is directed by Satan. The three and one-half years referred to by Daniel 7:25 is the second half of the Tribulation. The whole of his assignment is found in Revelation 13:7.

> ***"It was given unto him to make war with the saints, and to overcome them: and power was given him over all kindreds, and tongues, and nations."***
>
> ***—Revelation 13:7***

Authority was given to him over every tribe, tongue and nation. This is the verse of scripture that has been lifted totally out of context by theologians. This verse, Revelation 13:7, taken out of context, allows one to teach that the Antichrist will rule the world. Some teach that there will come a One World government ruled by the Antichrist. Leave this verse in context. Learn that this is the assignment that has been given to him by Satan, the dragon, the devil. It is not an assignment from God.

Revelation 13:7 is not revealing what he will do. It is revealing the assignment that Satan has given to him. We discover from God's Word his exact assignment. We learn from Daniel 8:24 that his power is not his own.

> ***"And his power shall be mighty, but not by his own power: and he shall destroy wonderfully, and shall prosper, and practice, and shall destroy the mighty and the holy people."***
>
> ***—Daniel 8:24***

Again, we must keep everything in context. The Antichrist is desperate in the last half of the Tribulation. Does he destroy all of the holy people? Does he execute everyone who has accepted the Lord Jesus Christ through the ministry of angels in the second half of the Tribulation? Absolutely not, only a small percentage of them. Please understand the Godly represent God on this earth, and the Lord Jesus Christ. They cannot be destroyed by Satan, regardless of what he attempts.

Satan has been trying for nearly 2,000 years to crush and destroy the Church. He has not done so. All his attempts have failed. The Church is once again gaining strength and momentum.

In spite of the fact that theologians do not always abide by their own rules and take scripture out of context; Satan fails to achieve his goal of world conquest.

The Biblical statements are crystal clear, the Antichrist gets his assignment from Satan, the dragon, and is opposed by God.

Various books on the subject of theology and Bible prophecy will declare a coming one world government ruled by the Antichrist. All are based on scripture taken out of context. Consider again Revelation 6:8.

> *"And I looked, and behold a pale horse: and his name that sat on him was Death, and Hell followed with him. And power was given unto them over the fourth part of the earth, to kill with sword, and with hunger, and with death, and with the beasts of the earth."*
>
> *—Revelation 6:8*

The last sentence in the verse states, "The four horsemen released as Jesus opens the first four seals have authority over only one-fourth of the earth."

Zechariah 14:16 offers confirmation.

> *"And it shall come to pass, that every one that is left of all the nations which came against Jerusalem shall*

***even go up from year to year to worship the King, the LORD of hosts, and to keep the feast of tabernacles."***
***—Zechariah 14:16***

God never contradicts Himself, but theologians do.

The prophet Zechariah identifies people from the nations over which the Antichrist has influential control, that do not hear him, do not follow him, do not take his mark, do not worship his image; and survive the Tribulation period, coming into the 1,000-year reign of our Lord.

In Revelation 5, Jesus is standing in front of the throne with the righteous that he has caught up from earth to heaven. He walks back to the throne and the father hands him a scroll that has seven seals upon it. He begins opening the seals. With the opening of the first seal, it releases the Antichrist to begin to carry out his satanic assignment.

He opens the second seal which releases the red horse, ridden by the man of war. In spite of the fact that the Antichrist will attempt to pass himself off as a man of peace, there is war throughout the seven-year period we know as the Tribulation.

By the way, Daniel reveals the followers of the Antichrist, declaring, "He destroys wonderfully." (Daniel 8:24)

Then the third seal is opened, and it releases the black horse whose rider causes famine to affect many parts of the earth. This is not an absence of food, this is a famine identified with a shortage, rather than a total absence.

> ***"And when he had opened the fourth seal, I heard the voice of the fourth beast say, Come and see."***
>
> ***—Revelation 6:7***

In verse 7, the fourth seal is opened by Jesus, releasing a pale horse. So the fourth horse of the Apocalypse, as they are sometimes referred to, is none other than the pale horse ridden by death, accompanied by hell.

We read in verse 8, ***"And the name of him who sat on it was Death; and hell followed with him."*** That verse ends with an amazing statement. Look in your Bible at the last sentence of verse 8. It will read the same in all of them. "And power was given to them…"

"…***over a fourth of the earth."*** Not the whole world. Your Bible does not support a coming One-world government, led by or ruled over by the Antichrist. However, we know from this same Bible that there is going to be a One World government when Jesus returns at the end of the Tribulation. World peace will then be the order of the day.

> ***"For unto us a child is born, unto us a son is given: and the government shall be upon his shoulder: and his name shall be called Wonderful, Counsellor, The mighty God, The everlasting Father, The Prince of Peace."***
>
> ***—Isaiah 9:6***

According to the prophecies of Isaiah 9:6, Jesus will take all the governments of the world upon His shoulders. Then, and then only, will we have a One World government that will be a theocracy. Jesus is going to rule and reign over all the nations of the world for 1,000 years in absolute peace and righteousness. But according to the scriptures, the Antichrist rules over only one-fourth of the earth for only seven years and they are filled with trouble for him.

Revelation 6:8b makes it completely clear that the Antichrist, man of war, famine and death affect only one-fourth of the earth, during the Tribulation.

Daniel, chapters 7 and 8, reveal his area of influence to be the European, Mediterranean and Middle Eastern area. He will not rule all of Europe nor Africa. He does not rule over the Orient, nor the Arab nations.

We learn from Revelation 9:13–16 that there will come a 200 million man army from the Orient with awesome military firepower against the Antichrist.

> *"And the sixth angel sounded, and I heard a voice from the four horns of the golden altar which is before God, Saying to the sixth angel which had the trumpet, Loose the four angels which are bound in the great river Euphrates. And the four angels were loosed, which were prepared for an hour, and a day, and a month, and a year, for to slay the third part of men. And the number of the army of the horsemen were two hundred thousand thousand: and I heard the number of them."*
>
> *—Revelation 9:13–16*

Daniel 11:44 tells us that the Antichrist will hear of reports coming out of the East, that's the Orient.

> *"But tidings out of the east and out of the north shall trouble him: therefore he shall go forth with great fury to destroy, and utterly to make away many."*
>
> *—Daniel 11:44*

It will trouble him. I suppose so, if there is a 200 million-man army marching in your direction with the most awesome military firepower in all of history! You would also be troubled.

What we are discovering is that he has no authority in the Orient. We know from Isaiah 19 and Zechariah 14 that he has no authority in the world of the Arabs. The Arabs will not bow down to him. They will not accept or follow him. The Arab nations are here during the millennial reign of our Lord Jesus Christ, serving Him, along with all other nations.

> *"In that day shall there be a highway out of Egypt to Assyria, and the Assyrian shall come into Egypt, and the Egyptian into Assyria, and the Egyptians shall serve with the Assyrians. In that day shall Israel be the third with Egypt and with Assyria, even a blessing in the midst of the land: Whom the LORD of hosts shall*

> ***bless, saying, Blessed be Egypt my people, and Assyria the work of my hands, and Israel mine inheritance."***
>
> ***—Isaiah 19:23–25***

Descendants from Abraham, through Ishmael, will accept our Lord Jesus Christ. Since it is prophesied in the Word of God that is the way it will be!

## The Wilderness

We learn from Revelation 12, in the last three and one-half years of the Tribulation, the unsaved remnant of the Jewish population will be hidden away in a wilderness that is populated. The population there has more than enough to feed them, to minister to them, and to take care of all of their needs.

This information would identify yet another part of our planet that the Antichrist does not rule over. We have discovered from the Word of God that the Antichrist does not rule the world as traditional theology declares.

## Tools of the Antichrist

What are some of the tools the Antichrist must use? Television. Since he is going to attempt to have a worldwide audience, the

Antichrist is certainly going to need television. Is television perfected today? Absolutely. Uplinks, downlinks, satellites and live streaming over the Internet.

The first time a worldwide audience was addressed via satellite television was in 1981. Kenneth Copeland, from his Southwest Believers Conference in Ft. Worth, Texas, brought in sufficient electronic technicians to tie all of the existing satellites of that day together for a worldwide communion service. ABC, NBC and CBS were there, wanting to find out how he did it. Thank God the righteous were the first to do it.

Isn't the advance in technology amazing? In fact, it is astronomical. In only 50–60 years we have rapidly advanced from elementary to highly sophisticated technology. Consider the rapid improvement in automotive, aviation, computer, space and electronic technology in only 50 years.

The future of technology seems, at the moment, unrestricted. According to Boeing Aircraft, we will soon be flying from city to city close to the speed of sound, about 750 miles per hour.

Approximately 600 years before the birth of Jesus, God prophesied through Daniel that knowledge would increase.

> ***"And at that time shall Michael stand up, the great prince which standeth for the children of thy people:***

> *and there shall be a time of trouble, such as never was since there was a nation even to that same time: and at that time thy people shall be delivered, every one that shall be found written in the book. And many of them that sleep in the dust of the earth shall awake, some to everlasting life, and some to shame and everlasting contempt. And they that be wise shall shine as the brightness of the firmament; and they that turn many to righteousness as the stars forever and ever. But thou, O Daniel, shut up the words, and seal the book, even to the time of the end: many shall run to and fro, and knowledge shall be increased."*
>
> *—Daniel 12:1–4*

The increase of knowledge and man's ability to quickly roam the earth are signs of the "time of the end." By the way, this phrase "time of the end" is not a term of doom and gloom. It simply means "Thank God it is Friday!"

The time of the end is the conclusion of the last days. The last days date back to Jesus and we are now in the closing of that frame of time. For the community of Christians who follow Jesus, we have entered the last day of our spiritual work week. Friday is always a feverish day of activity for the secular world, and so this should be our greatest hour of evangelism.

According to Daniel 12:1–4, the "time of the end" begins with the people of Daniel (Jewish people) surviving the holocaust of World War Two and are once again back in their homeland.

The end time got underway with the rebirth of Israel in 1948. We know we are in the time of the end as man's ability to travel anywhere on the earth, in a matter of hours, is improving.

Since the 1950s satellites, uplinks, downlinks have reached a higher degree of perfection than ever before. Does that make television of the Antichrist? No, it certainly does not. There is nothing wrong with television except the godless programming that is produced by the networks. One should be careful not to fill their mind with the godless, corrupt, violent, immoral programming of ABC, NBC, CBS, CNN, FOX and others. Keep your minds clear of television trash. Think on those things that are pure and upright and holy.

> ***"Finally, brethren, whatsoever things are true, whatsoever things are honest, whatsoever things are just, whatsoever things are pure, whatsoever things are lovely,***

> ***whatsoever things are of good report; if there be any virtue, and if there be any praise, think on these things."***
>
> ***—Philippians 4:8***

Television and technology will become tools for the Antichrist. What else will he use? Radio. His message will go out not only by television but by radio as well. What is the state of radio today? Radio is widespread, worldwide.

Is there another available tool? Yes, computers. Does this make computers of the Antichrist? No. A report went out some years ago, of a giant computer in Brussels, Belgium called "the beast." That story circulated in the Christian community like ***"a brush fire in a dry thicket fanned by a strong wind."***

I took the time and the necessary expense to fly to New York and visit IBM to discuss this with them. They knew all about that story. They chuckled and said to me, ***"You are much too intelligent and knowledgeable to accept this story."*** I said, ***"I haven't. I have come here to get information from you that I cannot get from any other source."*** Their explanation was that such a huge computer would never give a printout. A computer of that size would be checking itself out all day long. It would never produce a finished report. Then they pointed out that computers are getting smaller. Microchips are getting smaller, not larger.

Stop allowing the devil to deceive and mislead you. Some Christians see the mark of the beast in many things and just know the Antichrist is right outside. Do not be gullible. Be Word taught and correctly informed.

Computers enable us to communicate with one another much more rapidly and directly than ever before. It is a wonderful tool to help spread the gospel.

What else will the Antichrist have need of? The military. According to the Word of God, he does have military. The Old Testament bears that out and the New Testament as well, particularly from the seventeenth chapter of Revelation.

He will be in control of the armies of the European nations which support him. Their leaders will have pledged their allegiance to him, and have placed their armies under his authority. He will use his military might in taking over the city of Jerusalem and parts of the Middle East.

He intends to conquer the world. Among his many problems is Jesus who returns at the end of the Tribulation. The armies of the Antichrist are totally destroyed in one hour at the battle of Armageddon. The Antichrist and the False

Prophet are captured alive and cast into the Lake of Fire to be punished forever.

## NOT A DEATHBLOW

Traditional theology teaches that the Antichrist will be assassinated during the Tribulation and the False Prophet will resurrect him. There is no truth in such teaching. Remember that the Antichrist is a human being. Were he struck a deathblow, he would die and immediately go to hell. Remember Hebrews 9:27 *NKJ,* in which Paul says, ***"And as it is appointed for men to die once, but after this the judgment."***

Please understand the False Prophet could not resurrect him even if he tried. Resurrection power is resident only in God the Father, God the Son and God the Holy Ghost, and Believers when it becomes necessary for them to raise someone from the dead. This is rare, but there are occasions in which a Believer has had the anointing to raise the dead.

Resurrection power does not reside with Satan or any of his forces. The False Prophet cannot resurrect a dead Antichrist, nor does he just make it appear he is alive. We have learned from Revelation 19 that the False Prophet and the Antichrist are cast alive into the Lake of Fire. If he were actually dead, he would have to be resurrected to be cast alive into the Lake of Fire and the False Prophet does not possess such power.

Remember our insight concerning the Antichrist comes only from God's Word. This is not human speculation or opinion. How wonderful to discover what the Word of God has to say about the Antichrist.

# Opposition to Him During the Tribulation

*"He causes all, both small and great,*
*rich and poor, free and slave,*
*to receive a mark on their right*
*hand or on their foreheads."*

*—Revelation 13:16 NKJ*

CHAPTER FIVE

# Opposition to Him During the Tribulation

God is and always has been the God of divine order. His eternal plan is orderly and every event from beginning to eternity is fixed in place. Only Satan has attempted to circumvent God's order and plan. He has caused problems but has had no measure of success.

His greatest attempt is yet to come during the seven years of Tribulation. Even then Satan's defeat is thorough and the triumph of God through Jesus is awesome.

God's orderly plan and its events are all well-placed in His "textbook," the Bible, God's Word.

The prophesied event of the appearing of Jesus, to catch away the righteous, is the only one whose exact time is not revealed. However, the season in which the event will occur is known. We are now in that season.

Without the departure of the righteous Old Testament saints and the Church, the day of Christ coming to reign on the earth cannot begin. What else? The righteous must be caught up first, then the "man of sin," the Antichrist is revealed. Do you have these truths in divine order? Let's find out if this order is correct.

II Thessalonians 2:5 *NKJ*, ***"Do you not remember that when I was still with you I told you these things?"*** Paul is reminding the Thessalonians that he had taught them correctly, but they had permitted someone to come after him and bring confusion by teaching what is not true. I have encountered people who say, ***"Well, I used to believe in the Rapture before the Tribulation. I don't believe that anymore because I have heard it taught that the Church has to go through the Tribulation and it seems logical to me."***

I never cease being amazed at how little scripture most Christians know. From Genesis to Revelation the Bible places the catching away of the righteous before the Tribulation. Please reference my book entitled, "The Next Resurrection—You May Never Die."

The Word of God does not create confusion. Paul states in 1 Corinthians 14:33, God is not the author of confusion.

## OPPOSITION TO HIM DURING THE TRIBULATION

> ***"For God is not the author of confusion, but of peace, as in all churches of the saints."***
>
> ***—1 Corinthians 14:33***

When confusion is evident, Satan has been at work. In fact, he has sown more confusion about the catching away of the Church and the Book of Revelation than all other scriptures combined. Sometimes ministers aid him by parroting his erroneous theology.

II Thessalonians 2:3, begins ***"Let no one deceive you by any means,"*** especially theological confusion. You are safe and correct when you stay with the Bible. Verse 5 of II Thessalonians 2 continues ***"Do you not remember that when I was still with you I told you these things*** **(in other words I taught you correctly)** ***and now you know what is restraining, that he*** **(in reference to the Antichrist)** ***may be revealed in his own time."*** Verse 3 says he has to be ***"revealed:"*** verse 6 says he has to be ***"revealed in his time." "His time"*** is a fixed period of exactly seven years.

He cannot be revealed before that seven-year period is ready to begin, and that seven-year period cannot begin until the Church has been caught away. This is the divine order established within the Holy Scriptures. Revelation, chapter five, describes Jesus standing before the throne, surrounded by His company. In chronological order he opens the first seal of the scroll in Chapter six and releases the Antichrist.

Again, the Antichrist cannot be revealed as long as the Church is present on earth. Satan has attempted to bring forth this plan on numerous occasions and he has always failed either because God hindered it, or because of the presence of the Church.

Let us now examine the opposition to the Antichrist throughout the seven-year period of the Tribulation.

### First Half of Tribulation

The first three and one-half years, 42 months, or 1,260 days, the Antichrist is opposed by 144,000 unmarried Jewish servants of God who carry out the same beautiful assignment that you and I, as God's people, are presently carrying out. That is, see to it that the Gospel is preached in every nation to every one.

The Church, the Body of Christ, has that responsibility right now. We are presently doing a fair job. However, we are going to do even better as the Church reaches full maturity, as taught by the Apostle Paul. Ephesians Chapters 4 and 5 are very prophetic. The Church matures, becomes a living image of Jesus and absolutely glorious before being caught away. Once the righteous are caught up to heaven, the 144,000 Jewish servants of God take our place. The 144,000 are thoroughly described for us in Revelation 7:1–8 and Revelation 14:1–5.

> *"And after these things I saw four angels standing on the four corners of the earth, holding the four winds of the earth, that the wind should not blow on the earth, nor on the sea, nor on any tree. And I saw another angel ascending from the east, having the seal of the living God: and he cried with a loud voice to the four angels, to whom it was given to hurt the earth and the sea, Saying, Hurt not the earth, neither the sea, nor the trees, till we have sealed the servants of our God in their foreheads. And I heard the number of them which were sealed: and there were sealed an hundred and forty and four thousand of all the tribes of the children of Israel. Of the tribe of Judah were sealed twelve thousand. Of the tribe of Reuben were sealed twelve thousand. Of the tribe of Gad were sealed twelve thousand. Of the tribe of Aser were sealed*

*twelve thousand. Of the tribe of Nepthalim were sealed twelve thousand. Of the tribe of Manasses were sealed twelve thousand. Of the tribe of Simeon were sealed twelve thousand. Of the tribe of Levi were sealed twelve thousand. Of the tribe of Issachar were sealed twelve thousand. Of the tribe of Zabulon were sealed twelve thousand. Of the tribe of Joseph were sealed twelve thousand. Of the tribe of Benjamin were sealed twelve thousand."*

*—Revelation 7:1–8*

*"And I looked, and, lo, a Lamb stood on the mount Sion, and with him an hundred forty and four thousand, having his Father's name written in their foreheads. And I heard a voice from heaven, as the voice of many waters, and as the voice of a great thunder: and I heard the voice of harpers harping with their harps: And they sung as it were a new song before the throne, and before the four beasts, and the elders: and no man could learn that song but the hundred and forty and four thousand, which were redeemed from the earth. These are they which were not defiled with women; for they are virgins. These are they which follow the Lamb*

> *whithersoever he goeth. These were redeemed from among men, being the firstfruits unto God and to the Lamb. And in their mouth was found no guile: for they are without fault before the throne of God."*
>
> *—Revelation 14:1–5*

These are the two Biblical references that identify and describe the 144,000.

We know there are 12,000 out of each of the 12 tribes of Israel making a total of 144,000. We also know they are called *"Servants of God."* A servant of God is one who has a divine assignment that must be carried out. We further understand they are sealed with the seal of God on their forehead. We get that information from Chapter 7 of Revelation. From Chapter 14, we discover that the seal is the Father's name. We also discover that they are unmarried, so they do not have to devote quality time, of each day, to their wife and children.

Those of us who are married and have children, and perhaps grandchildren, have a righteous responsibility for them. Therefore, we who are called into the ministry of our Lord Jesus Christ, cannot devote all of our waking hours to the ministry. We must devote quality time to our family.

Look at God's list of priorities: God wants himself to be first in your life, your family second, your ministry third, provided you are called, and the people to whom you minister, are fourth. So do not ever neglect your family for the sake of your ministry. If one does so, he is out of divine order.

From Revelation 14, we discover that the 144,000 are unmarried Jewish men that have been born again. They have been redeemed as it stated twice in the first five verses of Revelation chapter 14. It states they are the "firstfruits" to God and to the Lamb. They are the first ones to be born again by accepting Jesus, after the Glorious Church has been caught away. They, by the enablement of the Holy Spirit, take our place. The first five verses in Revelation 14 reveal that they are led by the Holy Spirit, as it clearly states they follow Jesus. See Romans 8:14.

There isn't any question that the Holy Spirit is still here during the Tribulation. He has not been removed, as some teach. We find numerous references to the presence of the Holy Spirit within the Book of Revelation. In fact, there are twice as many references to the Holy Spirit's presence and operation during the Tribulation than there are to the Antichrist and the False Prophet.

So the Holy Spirit is here carrying out his divine assignment during the Tribulation. He is anointing and empowering the 144,000. The seal of God on their forehead gives them divine immunization from any harm. This allows them to operate right under the nose of the Antichrist in the first three and one-half years of the Tribulation; and he cannot do one thing about it.

The servants of God, with the anointing of the Holy Spirit, together with the Antichrist's internal problems are more than he can handle.

The 144,000 finish their public ministry, during the first half of the Tribulation. Afterward they minister to the remnant of Israel, who as yet have not accepted Jesus as their Messiah. Once the remnant of Israel is worshipping not only the God of Abraham, Isaac and Jacob, but the Lord Jesus Christ, the 144,000, having finished their assignment, will be caught up from earth to heaven just as their converts were at mid-Tribulation. See Revelation 7:9–17.

## A Mighty Harvest of Souls

The 144,000 have an amazing harvest of souls. The description of the converts of their ministry, is found in Revelation 7:9–17.

*"After this I beheld, and, lo, a great multitude, which no man could number, of all nations, and kindreds, and people, and tongues, stood before the throne, and before the Lamb, clothed with white robes, and palms in their hands; And cried with a loud voice, saying, Salvation to our God which sitteth upon the throne, and unto the Lamb. And all the angels stood round about the throne, and about the elders and the four beasts, and fell before the throne on their faces, and worshipped God, Saying, Amen: Blessing, and glory, and wisdom, and thanksgiving, and honour, and power, and might, be unto our God for ever and ever. Amen.*

*And one of the elders answered, saying unto me, What are these which are arrayed in white robes? and whence came they? And I said unto him, Sir, thou knowest. And he said to me, These are they which came out of great tribulation, and have washed their robes, and made them white in the blood of the Lamb. Therefore are they before the throne of God, and serve him day and night in his temple: and he that sitteth on the throne shall dwell among them. They shall hunger no more, neither thirst any more; neither shall the sun light on them, nor any heat. For the Lamb which is in*

> ***the midst of the throne shall feed them, and shall lead them unto living fountains of waters: and God shall wipe away all tears from their eyes."***
>
> ***—Revelation 7:9–17***

Consider this huge harvest of souls from every nation, every race, every language, and dialect. The 144,000 are going to win a massive number of people to the Lord Jesus during the first half of the Tribulation. The Antichrist and his crowd can do absolutely nothing about it. What a tremendous harvest and triumph for God and Jesus.

The prophet Zechariah 8:23 also gives us insight into the harvest.

> ***"Thus saith the LORD of hosts; In those days it shall come to pass, that ten men shall take hold out of all languages of the nations, even shall take hold of the skirt of him that is a Jew, saying, We will go with you: for we have heard that God is with you."***
>
> ***—Zechariah 8:23***

He declares that for every Jewish person that accepts Jesus as Messiah, there will be ten times that many Gentile men from every nation. Their confession is, ***"We've heard that God is with you. We will go with you."***

No wonder that John writes in Rev. 7:9, ***"I saw a great multitude that no man could number, from every nation and race and tribe and language on this planet."*** They are raptured just as the Church was before the Tribulation; bodily and alive. This company is taken up to heaven just as the second half of the Tribulation is beginning. By this act they escape the wrath of God during the last 3 ½ years.

Is there other opposition to the Antichrist during the first half of the Tribulation? Absolutely! We have already touched on it, but let's briefly return to Daniel 7:20, 24:

> ***"And of the ten horns that were in his head, and of the other which came up, and before whom three fell; even of that horn that had eyes, and a mouth that spake very great things, whose look was more stout than his fellows. And the ten horns out of this kingdom are ten kings that shall arise: and another shall rise after them; and he shall be diverse from the first, and he shall subdue three kings.***
>
> ***—Daniel 7:20,24***

Three of the original European nations that have put the Antichrist in power, will rebel against him, necessitating that he put them down and reduce them from having authority in that organization any longer.

The internal opposition from these three nations causes considerable problems, forcing him to give serious attention to this upheaval. This is further reason why he can do nothing against the 144,000 and their Holy Spirit–anointed ministry.

## Opposition During the Second Half of the Tribulation

Revelation 13 provides vital information concerning the Antichrist and the False Prophet. The False Prophet introduces the mark of the beast to be placed either on the right hand or forehead. Some years ago, it was taught that this mark would be a tattoo. Today many think it to be a microchip implanted under the skin. Technology is advancing so rapidly that six months or a year from now there may be some new technological development more applicable than a microchip implanted under the skin. Daniel 12:4 prophesies this hour of exploding technology. It is a sign of the end time.

***"But thou, O Daniel, shut up the words, and seal the book, even to the time of the end: many shall run to and fro, and knowledge shall be increased."***

***—Daniel 12:4***

We cannot be dogmatic about what method the Antichrist, the False Prophet and their cohorts will use on those who are willing to accept his mark. Technology will have produced the proper method used to identify their followers. The threat is, if you don't have this mark, you cannot enter into any kind of commercial transaction. Control of commerce provides a powerful leverage; this is the reason for the Mark of the Beast.

At mid-Tribulation, the Antichrist and the False Prophet introduce the mark of the beast, which is the number ***"666."*** Please do not get caught up in formulas and theological reasoning as to what the mark of the beast may be. The scripture is quite clear. Revelation 13:18 *NKJ*, ***"Here is wisdom. Let him who has understanding*** **(and you do)** ***calculate the number of the beast, for it is the number of a man: his number is 666."***

Notice this simple statement. It cancels the struggle of trying to determine what the mark of the beast consists of. ***"…his number is 666."*** A more clear statement could not be made.

Notice there are only six verses of scripture that deal with the mark of the beast in the book of Revelation. It is not brought up anywhere else except in this book. The mark is not introduced until the middle of the Tribulation. The Antichrist is certainly going to use highly developed technology in the application of the mark.

If everyone took the mark of the beast, as some folks have taught, there would be no one left alive at the end of the Tribulation to produce the nations during the millennial reign of Christ. As one reads the Book of Revelation, the statement is clear that only those whose names are not written in the Lamb's Book of Life will worship the image and take the mark.

> ***"And all that dwell upon the earth shall worship him, whose names are not written in the book of life of the Lamb slain from the foundation of the world."***
>
> ***—Revelation 13:8***

True, some people confronted with the mark of the beast during the last half of the Tribulation take the mark, but not all of the people. This fact is established very clearly by those who reject the Antichrist due to divine intervention, as well as the Orientals, the Arab world, and the populated wilderness where the remnant of Israel is hidden from the Antichrist. (Revelation 12:14).

> ***"He causes all, both small and great, rich and poor, free and slave, to receive a mark on their right hand or on their foreheads."***
>
> ***—Revelation 13:16 NKJ***

The mark of the beast will identify a person within the system of the Antichrist and the False Prophet. Remember, this is their way of attempting to control commerce.

The worship of the image of the Beast is the new idolatrous religion established by the False Prophet for the remainder of the Tribulation.

## False Prophet

Prior to the Antichrist establishing headquarters in Jerusalem, he has a major partner. From Revelation 13, we get insight to this partner, the False Prophet. The False Prophet is without question a religious leader. Who might he be? I don't know. You will hear people speculate. They name this one or that one or another. I will not do so because I cannot, from the authority of the scripture, personally identify the one who is to become the False Prophet. Remember, speculation is not "Thus says the Lord!"

From the scripture we learn of his operation and his association with the Antichrist. Such a partnership provides the Antichrist a partner with a religious background who has great influence with masses of people. The Antichrist uses this arrangement to propel himself into a more commanding diplomatic position with religious overtures. After all, he does intend to announce himself god.

> *"Let no man deceive you by any means: for that day shall not come, except there come a falling away first, and that man of sin be revealed, the son of perdition; Who opposeth and exalteth himself above all that is called God, or that is worshipped; so that he as God sitteth in the temple of God, showing himself that he is God."*
>
> *—II Thessalonians 2:3–4*

You learn about the False Prophet beginning in Revelation 13:11 where John writes, *"Then I saw another beast coming up out of the earth, and he had two horns like a lamb and spoke like a dragon."* He looks like a lamb and speaks like a devil. In the truest sense, we can use an old term, he is a ***"wolf in sheep's clothing."*** He, the False Prophet, exercises all the authority of the first beast (the Antichrist). ***"And he exercises all the authority of the first beast in his presence, and causes the earth and those who dwell in it to worship the first beast, whose deadly wound was healed. He performs great signs, so that he even makes fire come down from heaven on the earth in the sight of men."*** (Rev. 13:12–13 *NKJ*) Remember Paul states in II Thessalonians 2:9, these are ***"lying signs and wonders."***

> ***"And he deceives those who dwell on the earth by those signs which he was granted to do in the sight of the beast, telling those who dwell on the earth to make an image to the beast who was wounded by the sword*** (military warfare) ***and lived."***
>
> ***—Revelation 13:14 NKJ***

This image is a statue with lifelike characteristics. It will not be a living entity, as you and I, but will have lifelike features. Such is not impossible today with the advancement of technology, particularly in the field of robotics. We now have robots that can carry on limited intellectual conversation. Technology for such an image is already in development.

Honda has introduced "Asimo," a robot that can walk and even go up and down stairs.

"Artificial Intelligence" a recent Hollywood production is based on the scientific world of robots working to create an intelligent robot.

The False Prophet introduces the worship of this image of the beast. The scriptures state he was granted power to give breath to the image. Who is it that is supporting these two? It is Satan, not God. God is not the one granting the Antichrist or the False Prophet anything. Daniel 8:24 and Revelation 13:2,4 clearly establish the Antichrist's and False Prophet's source as Satan.

> ***"He was granted power to give breath to the image of the beast, that the image of the beast should both speak and cause as many as would not worship the image of the beast to be killed."***
>
> ***—Revelation 13:15 NKJ***

This is the introduction of the ancient idolatry of Egypt. When we look back at Revelation 11:8 we discover that at mid-tribulation, when the Antichrist, the False Prophet and their following set up their headquarters in Jerusalem, the city will be known as Sodom and Egypt.

Does the Antichrist have opposition in the second half of the Tribulation? Absolutely! Once the 144,000 have finished their public ministry at the middle of the Tribulation, angels will begin the public ministry, Rev. 14:6–11.

> ***"And I saw another angel fly in the midst of heaven, having the everlasting gospel to preach unto them that dwell on the earth, and to every nation, and kindred, and tongue, and people,"***
>
> —***Revelation 14:6***

Notice the scripture states, angels preach ***"to every nation, tribe, tongue (language), and people."*** So at the middle of the Tribulation and throughout the remainder of that three and one-half year period, angels will be preaching to the people of every nation on this planet, and in their language. They will declare with a loud voice, ***"Fear God, and give glory to him, for the hour of his judgment has come; and worship him who made heaven and earth, the sea and springs of water."*** (verse 7)

The preaching of the Gospel is not going to stop when we Believers, are caught away. The 144,000 will continue preaching. The preaching of the Gospel is not going to end when they cease their public ministry. Angels take over the assignment. Notice as we read on, ***"And another angel followed saying,***

*'Babylon has fallen. That great city, because she has made all nations drink of the wine of the wrath for fornication.'"* (verse 8)

This identifies the Babylonian system of government, religion, and commerce, led by the Antichrist. This system, working in the first half of the Tribulation, is ended at mid-Tribulation when the Antichrist announces himself God. He and the False Prophet set their religion in place; and attempt, through the Mark of the Beast, to control commerce.

The angel declares the Babylonian system has fallen. Study the following verses,

> *"The third angel followed them, saying with a loud voice, If any man worship the beast and his image, and receive his mark in his forehead, or in his hand, The same shall drink of the wine of the wrath of God, which is poured out without mixture into the cup of his indignation; and he shall be tormented with fire and brimstone in the presence of the holy angels, and in the presence of the Lamb: And the smoke of their torment ascendeth up for ever and ever: and they have no rest day nor night, who worship the beast and his image, and whosoever receiveth the mark of his name."*
>
> *—Revelation 14:9–11*

Angels are declaring these truths to the whole world in the second half of the Tribulation. Here is divine opposition to the declaration of the Mark of the Beast and the introduction to the image of the Beast, the statue that appears to be alive.

How utterly awesome, angels immediately warning the people of the world not take the Mark of the Beast, or worship the image of the Beast. Should one do either, he or she would seal their doom in the Lake of Fire. There they are tormented with fire and brimstone, night and day, and have no rest for all eternity. What powerful opposition to the mark of the Beast and the worship of the image of the Beast. Angelic opposition to the Antichrist continues throughout the second half of the Tribulation.

Does he have any other opposition during the second half of the Tribulation? Yes, he does.

Opposition is coming out of the Orient. The great Oriental army that is described in Revelation, chapter 9, is advancing through the most densely populated areas of the world. They are destroying all opposition before them, on their way to do battle with the Antichrist.

This huge Oriental army is controlled by four fallen angels; demons under the authority of Satan. You may reason,

"But I thought the Antichrist was Satan's man?" He is, up until the sixth year of the Tribulation. By that time, it is evident he is a failure and will not succeed in carrying out the assignment that Satan has given to him.

So Satan then adopts "Plan B." Send the huge Oriental army, under the control of four fallen angels, to advance westward to the site of the Antichrist. However they do not fight each other. Both forces learn from the Two Witnesses that Jesus is within days of returning. In order to oppose His return, they join forces.

Therefore, the Antichrist with his armies, and the great Oriental army merge together. They will attempt to oppose the return of the Lord Jesus with his saintly armies. The action of the Antichrist and the Oriental army culminates in the Battle of Armageddon that takes only one hour. Jesus, speaking the Word of God on the Mount of Olives, releases the plague of Zechariah 14:12,

> *"And this shall be the plague wherewith the LORD will smite all the people that have fought against Jerusalem; Their flesh shall consume away while they stand upon their feet, and their eyes shall consume*

*away in their holes, and their tongue shall consume away in their mouth."*

*—Zechariah 14:12*

That huge armada in the Valley of Meggido will be reduced to utter destruction in only one hour, creating a pool of blood to the depth of a horse's bridle over an area of nearly 200 square miles as is described in Rev. 14:17–20:

*"And another angel came out of the temple which is in heaven, he also having a sharp sickle. And another angel came out from the altar, which had power over fire; and cried with a loud cry to him that had the sharp sickle, saying, Thrust in thy sharp sickle, and gather the clusters of the vine of the earth; for her grapes are fully ripe. And the angel thrust in his sickle into the earth, and gathered the vine of the earth, and cast it into the great winepress of the wrath of God. And the winepress was trodden without the city, and blood came out of the winepress, even unto the horse bridles, by the space of a thousand and six hundred furlongs."*

*—Revelation 14:17–20*

## OPPOSITION TO HIM DURING THE TRIBULATION

The Antichrist has awesome opposition during the second half of the Tribulation. The ministering angels, the threat of the Oriental army advancing on him out of the East; as well as the two witnesses of Revelation 11. The two witnesses prophesy in front of his headquarters every day. They provide an exact countdown as to how many days he has left before Jesus returns to cast him and the False Prophet, alive, into the Lake of Fire.

Throughout the seven-year period, known as the Tribulation, the Antichrist not only has divine opposition carried out by the 144,000, the angels and the two witnesses, but he has opposition from within and opposition from without. No wonder he is not able to successfully carry out the assignment that Satan has given him. Regardless of how resourceful, talented, and capable he is, he becomes an utter failure and is lost, for the cause of Satan.

# Present Day Opposition

*As long as the God-fearing righteous are here,*
*we are Christ's opposition to the Antichrist*
*and he cannot come forth. As long as*
*righteous are here there will*
*never be an Antichrist.*

Chapter Six

# Present Day Opposition

Opposition to the Antichrist is certainly powerful during the Tribulation. Today there is opposition to the spirit of the Antichrist through the righteous whether they recognize their authority or not. The presence of God fearing, Bible believing people prevents the revealing of the Antichrist.

The Apostle Paul's writings in II Thessalonians, chapter 2, identifies the spirit of the Antichrist operating in the world in his day. He identifies it as the spirit of "lawlessness" or "iniquity." The Antichrist Spirit has been present from then until today. In fact, it is awesomely evident.

> ***"For the mystery of iniquity doth already work: only he who now letteth will let, until he be taken out of the way. And then shall that Wicked be revealed, whom***

> *the Lord shall consume with the spirit of his mouth, and shall destroy with the brightness of his coming:"*
>
> *—II Thessalonians 2:7–8*

What do we know?

Satan is here in the world. See I Peter 5:8. He was here before the Church. He has been here throughout the time of the Church. So the presence of Satan provides the source of the spirit of the Antichrist.

The Apostle Paul recognized it. We ought also recognize it from the truth found in the Word of God. We must realize that we are in spiritual warfare. Spiritual warfare began when the anointed cherub, Lucifer, rebelled against God.

With the help of one-third of the angels, he attempted to overthrow God and unseat him. Michael and his angels defeated Lucifer and his angels, thoroughly; and cast them out of heaven to the earth (Luke 10:18; Revelation 12:9). Then God sent his only begotten Son that through believing in Him, and by his blood, mankind could overcome God's adversary, the devil. We now overcome him by the blood of the Lamb and the Word of our testimony (Revelation 12:11).

Satan, formerly Lucifer, the anointed cherub, has been cast down to the earth. Since the Church was established by our

Lord Jesus Christ and the Holy Spirit, we have been the divine opposition to Satan's plan.

When one parallels world history with the nearly 2,000 years of Church history, one discovers numerous attempts at world conquest.

Napoleon, Hitler, and others, are examples. There are, of course, others prior to their time. Were any who attempted to conquer the world Godly? No, not one! Were they agents of Satan? Yes! What was Satan attempting to do? He was attempting to bring forth this program of Antichrist. What prevented him from doing so? None other than the Body of Christ, which is identified by the Apostle Paul as the Church of which Jesus is the head.

Right now, the Church, the Body of Christ, born again of the Spirit of God, washed in the blood of the Lamb, anointed by the Holy Spirit, is the divine opposition to Satan, his plan and program in our world.

Satan cannot introduce the Antichrist as long as the Church remains on the earth. This Bible truth originates from the writings of the Apostle Paul in II Thessalonians, chapter 2.

It is evident from the information in II Thessalonians, chapter 2, that Paul recognized the spirit of the Antichrist as lawless and iniquity. He writes, "Only he who now restrains…." There was a divine restraining factor, in the day of Paul; preventing Satan from bringing forth his program. Such a program has to be headed by none other than the man who would become Antichrist.

***"Only he who now restrains will do so, until he is taken out of the way."*** The Apostle Paul is recognizing a divine restraining force in the world preventing Satan from introducing the Antichrist. This restrainer, or withholder, will continue to do so until he is taken out of the way. The restrainer is supernaturally removed. Then the lawless one will be revealed, whom the Lord will consume with the breath of His mouth, and destroy with the brightness of His coming.

The coming of the lawless one is according to the working of Satan, with all power, signs, and lying wonders; and all unrighteous deception among those who perish.

Who is this powerful restrainer?

Who is this awesome withholder?

Who was at work in Paul's day, whom he declares will continue to work as the restraining withholder of Satan's plan? A force so powerful, it does not allow Satan to introduce the Antichrist until he, the restrainer, has been taken out of the way.

Who is he who must be taken out of the way? None other than the anointed Church, the Body of Christ. Not the Holy Spirit, as traditional theology has taught us. We have already learned from the book of Revelation that the Holy Spirit is here throughout the Tribulation anointing the 144,000, anointing the Two Witnesses in Jerusalem, and certainly anointing the angels in the second half of the Tribulation.

> *"And it shall come to pass afterward, that I will pour out my spirit upon all flesh; and your sons and your daughters shall prophesy, your old men shall dream dreams, your young men shall see visions: And also upon the servants and upon the handmaids in those days will I pour out my spirit. And I will show wonders in the heavens and in the earth, blood, and fire, and pillars of smoke. The sun shall be turned into darkness, and the moon into blood, before the great and the terrible day of the LORD come. And it shall come to pass, that whosoever shall call on the name of the LORD shall be delivered: for in mount Zion and in Jerusalem shall be deliverance, as the LORD hath said, and in the remnant whom the LORD shall call."*
>
> *—Joel 2:28–32*

The prophet Joel, in the above scripture passages, causes us to understand that once the Holy Spirit began to be outpoured, that outpouring would continue right up until the last day of the Tribulation. The last day of the Tribulation is the day that the sun becomes darkened, the moon is as blood, and the powers of heaven are shaken. Jesus confirms this in Matthew 24:29.

> ***"Immediately after the tribulation of those days shall the sun be darkened, and the moon shall not give her light, and the stars shall fall from heaven, and the powers of the heavens shall be shaken:"***
>
> *—Matthew 24:29*

## Church to be Taken Away

We have confirmation from the Holy Scriptures that the Holy Spirit is still here, as he is today, throughout the Tribulation. Therefore the only restraining factor that is withholding Satan's plan, which must be taken out of the way, is the anointed Body of Christ, which the Scriptures identify as the Church. The scripture is exact, the true church must be removed in order for the Antichrist to be revealed. God has chosen to work through devout men and women to continue Satan's defeat.

You may ask, "Is there more than one Rapture?" Yes, we have already had three. We, the Church, are next. We are number four. The great multitude of Revelation, Chapter 7 is number five. When the 144,000 have absolutely finished all of their earthly assignment, they, too, are taken bodily and alive from earth to heaven which is rapture number six.

On the last day of the Tribulation, the two witnesses who have ministered in Jerusalem for three and one-half years are caught up from earth to heaven, making seven catching ups...God's perfect number. Some people have trouble believing there is going to be one Rapture, when there are seven.

1. ENOCH—before the flood in Genesis, chapter 5.
2. ELIJAH—The Prophet. 2 Kings, chapter 2.
3. JESUS—Acts, chapter one.
4. THE BODY OF CHRIST—Church and Old Testament saints. (I Thessalonians 4:16–18)
5. GREAT MULTITUDE—Revelation 7:9–17
6. 144,000—Early in the second half of the Tribulation (Revelation 14:5)
7. TWO WITNESSES—Last day of Tribulation (Revelation 11:12)

## Divine Opposition

The Church is presently the divine, earthly opposition to Satan; 24 hours a day, seven days a week. We, through Biblical instruction and by the anointing of the Holy Spirit, are preventing Satan from bringing forth his best program and introducing the Antichrist. Satan has opposition he cannot overcome; and he will never overcome it. Thank God for the truth and authority of the Word of God.

As long as the God-fearing righteous are here, we are Christ's opposition to the Antichrist and he cannot come forth. As long as righteous are here there will never be an Antichrist. The Tribulation events do not begin until Jesus opens the first seal, as we have studied, in Revelation 6:1–2. The ceremony of the opening of the seals follows the arrival of the righteous in heaven.

Paul reveals in II Thessalonians 2:3,6–8 that the Antichrist must be revealed. However, he cannot be until the Church has been taken out of the way. Then, and only then, can the Antichrist be revealed.

**Divine opposition to the Antichrist.** Presently, the Church is holding him back, and will continue to do so until the Church is taken out of the way at the appearance of Jesus.

However, the Church is not taken out of the way until it has become glorious and produces a huge harvest of souls.

The Antichrist is helpless to do anything about divine opposition. There will be tremendous soulwinning results and unhindered ministry throughout the seven years of the Tribulation.

# Why the Church Restrains Satan's Plan and How

*"Finally, my brethren, be strong in the Lord*
*and in the power of His might.*
*Put on the whole armor of God,*
*that you may be able to stand against*
*the wiles of the devil."*

*Ephesians 6:10–11*

## Chapter Seven

# Why the Church Restrains Satan's Plan and How

A. Church is "Body of Christ"—Kingdom of God on the earth—carrying on in Christ's stead

B. The Church has Divine Ability and Authority.

This Good News helps us to understand the importance of the assignment God has given to Believers. The divine task must be carried out with excellence and expediency. From today until the Rapture, the Church is God's **divine opposition to the Antichrist.** In II Thessalonians 2:7, Paul identifies the Church as "He," who must be taken out of the way.

Because traditional theology has long declared the Church to be the "Bride of Christ," you may have problems with the Church being "He." You should not, when all through the epistles of Paul the Church is always identified as the Body of Christ of which Christ is the Head. The terms "Church" and "Body of Christ" are interchangeable.

## THE CHURCH IS NOT THE BRIDE

Is it possible to harmonize the theology which states, "The Church is the Bride of Christ," with the Bible? There is not a single verse in the Bible that says the Church is the Bride of Christ. If you have been taught this all your life and you believe it, then you must know the verses of scripture that prove it. The Apostle Paul is very careful to teach both identity and relationship. When he teaches relationship he will use the example of the relationship between husband and wife. He is not teaching that the Church will be the bride of Christ. Your identity is crystal clear. You are the Body of Christ of which He is the Head. That makes you part of the Bridegroom not the Bride.

Carefully study Ephesians 4:11–16.

*"And he gave some, apostles; and some, prophets; and some, evangelists; and some, pastors and teachers; For the perfecting of the saints, for the work of the ministry, for the edifying of the body of Christ: Till we all come in the unity of the faith, and of the knowledge of the Son of God, unto a perfect man, unto the measure of the stature of the fullness of Christ: That we henceforth be no more children, tossed to and fro, and carried about with every wind of doctrine, by the sleight of men, and cunning craftiness, whereby they lie in wait to deceive; But speaking the truth in love, may grow up into him in all things, which is the head, even Christ: From whom the whole body fitly joined together and compacted by that which every joint supplieth, according to the effectual working in the measure of every part, maketh increase of the body unto the edifying of itself in love."*

*—Ephesians 4:11–16*

Paul clearly establishes the Church as a "perfect man." In Ephesians 5, theologians and publishers have inserted the word "her" instead of "it" in verses 25, 26 and 27. Had they simply used the word "it" they would not have contradicted the Apostle Paul, and been consistent with the original Greek text.

What does the Church wear? Armor. Ephesians 6:10–11, ***"Finally, my brethren, be strong in the Lord and in the power of His might. Put on the whole armor of God, that you may be able to stand against the wiles of the devil."*** That word ***"against"*** implies ***"attack."*** The armor of God is not designed only for defense. It is also designed for one to be on the attack. Also see James 4:7.

II Corinthians 10:4 says, ***"For the weapons of our warfare are not carnal but mighty in God for pulling down strongholds."*** We wear armor and use weapons. In Paul's writings to Timothy he told Timothy he was a soldier and to conduct himself as a soldier and not be overly involved in civilian activities. II Timothy 2:3. Now are we God's army in the world. As God's army, equipped with God's armor, using God's weapons, we are preventing the devil from bringing forth his best plan. It is not because he hasn't tried, but he cannot because the Church is here and is too powerful!

Please allow the Holy Bible and the Holy Spirit to teach the correct identity of a born again Christian and the relationship our spirits have with Jesus Christ. We have many confused Christians that have identity and relationship crossed. As long as this is the case, they will have difficulty receiving everything God has provided for them. The Epistles of Paul accurately teach the Church is the Body of Christ and not His Bride.

Paul also teaches that all followers of Jesus should develop the kind of relationship that allows Jesus to become the Lord of their life. Such a relationship is a divine intimacy. You are also God's military personnel in a battle with the devil over the souls of men.

> ***"Yet I supposed it necessary to send to you Epaphroditus, my brother, and companion in labour, and fellowsoldier, but your messenger, and he that ministered to my wants."***
>
> ***—Philippians 2:25***

> ***"Thou therefore endure hardness, as a good soldier of Jesus Christ. 4No man that warreth entangleth himself with the affairs of this life; that he may please him who hath chosen him to be a soldier."***
>
> ***—II Timothy 2:3–4***

> ***"And to our beloved Apphia, and Archippus our fellowsoldier, and to the church in thy house:"***
>
> ***—Philemon 2***

Who then is the Bride of Christ?

If it is not the Church, then who? In Ephesians, chapter five, Paul teaches relationship using the illustration of the husband and wife. His emphasis is on divine order and by no means is he identifying the Church as the Bride of Christ. The wise virgins of Matthew 25 were friends of the Bridegroom going to the wedding where the Bride was awaiting them. They were not the Bride.

In Revelation 21:9, an angel speaks to John (John is a member of the Church just like you and I), ***"Come, I will show you the bride, the Lamb's wife."***

Read carefully Revelation Chapter 19:1–10. The wedding of the Lamb follows after his bride has been made ready. She is adorned by the righteous acts of the saints; you, I, and the righteous company in heaven.

Revelation 21:1–10 identifies the Lamb's wife as the New Jerusalem. Please do not question God's Word. Simply by faith accept this truth. I never cease being amazed at how we allow our traditions to resist the actual statement of the Holy Scriptures.

**There are three huge harvests:**

1. THE END TIME HARVEST brought in by the Church.

*"And it shall come to pass in the last days, that the mountain of the LORD'S house shall be established in the top of the mountains, and shall be exalted above the hills; and all nations shall flow unto it."*
—*Isaiah 2:2*

*"But in the last days it shall come to pass, that the mountain of the house of the LORD shall be established in the top of the mountains, and it shall be exalted above the hills; and people shall flow unto it."*
—*Micah 4:1*

*"And they that be wise shall shine as the brightness of the firmament; and they that turn many to righteousness as the stars for ever and ever."*
—*Daniel 12:3*

*"Then said he unto him, A certain man made a great supper, and bade many: And sent his servant at supper time to say to them that were bidden, Come; for all things are now ready. And they all with one consent began to make excuse. The first said unto him, I have bought a piece of ground, and I must needs go and see it: I pray thee have me excused. And another said, I have bought five yoke of oxen, and I go to prove them: I pray thee have me excused. And another said, I have married a wife, and therefore I cannot come. So that servant came, and showed his lord these things. Then the master of the house being angry said to his servant, Go out quickly into the streets and lanes of the city, and bring in hither the poor, and the maimed, and the halt, and the blind. And the servant said, Lord, it is done as thou hast commanded, and yet there is room. And the lord said unto the servant, Go out into the highways and hedges, and compel them to come in, that my house may be filled.*

*—Luke 14:16–23*

2. The harvest brought in by the 144,000. See Revelation 7:9–17.
3. The harvest brought in by the angels. See Revelation 14:6–7, 14–16.

Jesus states in Luke 14 that His Father's house would be full. Heaven is a huge place and it will take a massive number of people to fill it.

The prophets Isaiah and Micah both prophesy a massive harvest of souls from all nations in the Last Days. Isaiah 2:2 and Micah 4:1 proclaim this prior to introducing the reign of our Lord Jesus. Daniel 12:3 also agrees when he writes of the wise, righteous ones turning MANY to righteousness at the time of the end. Also consider Proverbs 11:30.

Daniel 2:28–44 establishes God's Kingdom filling the whole earth in the Last Days...that means even before the return of Jesus with all His saints.

> ***"But there is a God in heaven that revealeth secrets, and maketh known to the king Nebuchadnezzar what shall be in the latter days. Thy dream, and the visions of thy***

*head upon thy bed, are these; As for thee, O king, thy thoughts came into thy mind upon thy bed, what should come to pass hereafter: and he that revealeth secrets maketh known to thee what shall come to pass. But as for me, this secret is not revealed to me for any wisdom that I have more than any living, but for their sakes that shall make known the interpretation to the king, and that thou mightest know the thoughts of thy heart.*

*Thou, O king, sawest, and behold a great image. This great image, whose brightness was excellent, stood before thee; and the form thereof was terrible. This image's head was of fine gold, his breast and his arms of silver, his belly and his thighs of brass, His legs of iron, his feet part of iron and part of clay. Thou sawest till that a stone was cut out without hands, which smote the image upon his feet that were of iron and clay, and brake them to pieces. Then was the iron, the clay, the brass, the silver, and the gold, broken to pieces together, and became like the chaff of the summer threshing-floors; and the wind carried them away, that no place was found for them: and the stone that smote the image became a great mountain, and filled the whole earth. This is the dream; and we will tell the interpretation thereof before the king. Thou, O king, art a king of kings: for the God of heaven hath given thee a kingdom, power, and strength, and glory. And wheresoever the children of men dwell, the beasts of the field and the fowls of the heaven hath he given into thine hand, and hath made thee ruler over them all. Thou art this head of gold. And after thee shall arise another kingdom inferior to thee, and another third kingdom of brass, which shall bear rule over all the earth. And the fourth kingdom shall be strong as iron: forasmuch as iron breaketh in pieces and subdueth all things: and as iron that breaketh all these, shall it break in pieces and bruise. And whereas thou sawest the feet and toes, part of potters' clay, and part of iron, the kingdom shall be divided; but there shall be in it of the strength of the iron, forasmuch as thou sawest the iron mixed with miry clay. And as the toes of the feet were part of iron, and part of clay, so the kingdom shall be partly strong, and partly broken. And whereas thou sawest iron mixed with miry clay, they shall mingle themselves with the seed of men: but they shall not cleave one to another, even as iron is not mixed with clay. And in the days of these kings shall the God of heaven set up a kingdom, which shall never*

> ***be destroyed: and the kingdom shall not be left to other people, but it shall break in pieces and consume all these kingdoms, and it shall stand for ever."***
>
> ***—Daniel 2:28–44***

The term "time of the end" simply means "Thank God it's Friday"—the last day of the Church's work week.

Soulwinning is the major priority of the Church. The responsibility of sharing the Gospel rests on the shoulders of each and every Believer. We are designated "soul winners." Both Solomon and Daniel address the wise as those who win souls. Are you wise? If so, you're winning souls.

The Holy Spirit was given so every Believer could be a witness of Jesus, at any time or place.

> ***"But ye shall receive power, after that the Holy Ghost is come upon you: and ye shall be witnesses unto me both in Jerusalem, and in all Judaea, and in Samaria, and unto the uttermost part of the earth."***
>
> ***—Acts 1:8***

Not only does Jesus declare his Father's house will be full, but Paul states in Ephesians 4:11–16 how it will occur. The

Body of Christ becomes so mature and anointed that multitudes are added daily to the Church.

Jesus makes a very profound statement:

> ***"Who then is a faithful and wise servant, whom his lord hath made ruler over his household, to give them meat in due season? Blessed is that servant, whom his lord when he cometh shall find so doing."***
>
> ***—Matthew 24:45–46***

He clearly expects to find you and me, His servants, doing what He has instructed—winning souls!

The most important priority of all is "Soul Winning"! In this vital category of souls, God is not going to lose to Satan. He gave His only begotten Son for all and it is not His will that any perish (II Peter 3:9). Furthermore, He sent the Holy Spirit to see to the absolute success of the Church.

The empowered Church will prevent the revealing of the Antichrist until it is taken out of the way. This is divine opposition to Satan and his plan.

Always keep in mind:

1. God's Armor

*"Finally, my brethren, be strong in the Lord, and in the power of his might. Put on the whole armor of God, that you may be able to stand against the wiles of the devil."*

*—Ephesians 6:10–11*

2. God's Weapons

*"(For the weapons of our warfare are not carnal, but mighty through God to the pulling down of strong holds;) Casting down imaginations, and every high thing that exalteth itself against the knowledge of God, and bringing into captivity every thought to the obedience of Christ;"*

*—II Corinthians 10:4–5*

3. Jesus the Head of the Church

*"But speaking the truth in love, may grow up into him in all things, which is the head, even Christ:"*

*—Ephesians 4:15*

> ***"For the husband is the head of the wife, even as Christ is the head of the church: and he is the saviour of the body."***
>
> ***—Ephesians 5:23***

He builds His Church –

> ***"And I say also unto thee, That thou art Peter, and upon this rock I will build my church; and the gates of hell shall not prevail against it."***
>
> ***—Matthew 16:18***

Satan is NOT victorious. He has suffered one defeat after another since Jesus came down from the Mount of Temptation. See Matthew 4:1–11.

4. Holy Spirit Anointing—The Other Helper

The End Time Church is to have twice the anointing of the Early Church. See Joel 2:23.

# Victory, not Fear!

*"God has not given us a spirit of fear,*

*but of power, of love, and of*

*a sound mind."*

*—II Timothy 1:7 NKJ*

## Chapter Eight

# Victory, Not Fear!

The book of Revelation is an amazing book of extremely important information. The more knowledge you have, the less fear can trouble you, and the less you are tormented and disturbed about events of the present and future. I have no fear of the Antichrist, the False Prophet, the mark of the beast or of the Tribulation Period because I know what the Word of God declares. Jesus states, ***"You shall know the truth and the truth shall make you free."*** (John 8:32 *NKJ*)

In Revelation 13:7, the assignment given to the Antichrist by Satan is to have power over all nations and make war against the Saints, but remember that is a satanic assignment. Is God going to allow him to succeed? No, God is not! God stated long ago in Psalms 24:1, ***"The earth is the Lord's, and all its fullness, The world and those who dwell therein."*** *NKJ* You cannot find a verse in the Word where God ever gives away or allows the devil to take it from Him. Satan is our defeated foe. Since God's majestic book provides no victory or success for Satan or his plan, neither should we.

The proper study of the prophecies of the scriptures produce hope, NOT fear. Thank God for hope. Hope ranks right along with faith and love. Don't drop hope down to a lower position. Keep it where God placed it in I Corinthians 13.

Proverbs 13:12 states, "Hope deferred makes the heart sick, but when the desire comes, it is a tree of life." *NKJ*

## Antichrist Is Defeated in Battle

As we study the scriptures, it reveals Satan's best plan. God, through men and angels, super-naturally destroys it. The Antichrist and his armies are defeated at the Battle of Armageddon. The Antichrist has a combined army from ten European nations. Zechariah 14 and Revelation 9 and 19 give you insight to the armies that will be following the Antichrist.

At the Battle of Armageddon the two armies of the Antichrist are combined with the two-hundred million Oriental army as revealed in Revelation Chapters 9 and 16. Together they resist the return of Jesus to the earth. All are destroyed in one hour on the last day of that seven-year period known as the Tribulation.

Zechariah 14 and Revelation 19 are major references pertaining to the return of Jesus and the utter defeat of the Antichrist. Once the armies of the Antichrist are totally destroyed, then the Antichrist and the False Prophet are cast alive into the Lake of Fire, as is recorded in Revelation 19.

> *"And I saw heaven opened, and behold a white horse; and he that sat upon him was called Faithful and True, and in righteousness he doth judge and make war. His eyes were as a flame of fire, and on his head were many crowns; and he had a name written, that no man knew, but he himself. And he was clothed with a vesture dipped in blood: and his name is called The Word of God. And the armies which were in heaven followed him upon white horses, clothed in fine linen, white and clean. And out of his mouth goeth a sharp sword, that with it he should smite the nations: and he shall rule them with a rod of iron: and he treadeth the winepress of the fierceness and wrath of Almighty God. And he hath on his vesture and on his thigh a name written, KING OF KINGS, AND LORD OF*

*LORDS. And I saw an angel standing in the sun; and he cried with a loud voice, saying to all the fowls that fly in the midst of heaven, Come and gather yourselves together unto the supper of the great God; That ye may eat the flesh of kings, and the flesh of captains, and the flesh of mighty men, and the flesh of horses, and of them that sit on them, and the flesh of all men, both free and bond, both small and great. And I saw the beast, and the kings of the earth, and their armies, gathered together to make war against him that sat on the horse, and against his army."*

*—Revelation 19:11–19*

## BATTLE OF ARMAGEDDON

Once the ceremonies and events in heaven are complete, Revelation 19:11 reveals Jesus is ready to step out of heaven and come back to the earth to reign for a thousand years. When Jesus rides out of heaven and returns to the earth, look at those accompanying Him, ***"And the armies in heaven, clothed in fine linen, white and clean, followed Him on white horses."***

The who? The armies. Who makes up His army? Zechariah 14:5 and Revelation 19:14 identify this vast company as a saintly army. Remember they wear armor, use weapons and are called soldiers. This is also the description of the righteous prior to their ascension to heaven. Seven years later, at the end of the Tribulation when this same company comes back with Jesus to reign, they are still His army, not His Bride.

Once the righteous Church has been caught away and are in heaven, someone else has to preach the gospel in order for people to have the opportunity of salvation.

We understand that for mankind to be saved, Jesus has to be preached. This truth is established by the Apostle Paul in Romans 10:13–17. Peter agrees with John 3:16 when he writes it is not God's will ***"that any should perish but that all should come to repentance."*** (II Peter 3:9) For mankind to come to repentance, the gospel has to be preached.

We were taught, by well-meaning teachers, years ago that once the Church was caught away, no one could be saved following the Rapture. Then after a number of years, the teaching was modified because of prophecies in Zechariah, chapter 8:23 and Romans 11:25–27.

> ***"Thus saith the LORD of hosts; In those days it shall come to pass, that ten men shall take hold out of all languages of the nations, even shall take hold of the***

*skirt of him that is a Jew, saying, We will go with you: for we have heard that God is with you."*

*—Zechariah 8:23*

*"For I would not, brethren, that ye should be ignorant of this mystery, lest ye should be wise in your own conceits; that blindness in part is happened to Israel, until the fulness of the Gentiles be come in. And so all Israel shall be saved: as it is written, There shall come out of Sion the Deliverer, and shall turn away ungodliness from Jacob: For this is my covenant unto them, when I shall take away their sins."*

*—Romans 11:25–27*

Theologians and teachers decided Jews could get saved because Paul had prophesied in Romans 11 that all Israel would be saved. However, they were still quite adamant that no Gentiles could be saved during the Tribulation. Considering the many references to God's mercy and love, that was strange doctrine. Once the Church has been caught away, Revelation 7 reveals God does replace the Church with the 144,000 for the preaching of the gospel to every nation, tribe, people, and tongue. Jews and Gentiles can be saved during the Tribulation.

*"For God so loved the world that He gave His only begotten Son, that whoever believes in Him should not perish but have everlasting life." John 3:16 NKJ*

Once the Tribulation runs its course, the Antichrist and False Prophet are captured, their armada is destroyed, and they are cast alive into the Lake of Fire. There they are to be tormented forever, *"And the beast was taken, and with him the false prophet that wrought miracles before him, with which he deceived them that had received the mark of the beast, and them that worshipped his image. These both were cast alive into a lake of fire burning with brimstone. And the remnant were slain with the sword of him that sat upon the horse, which sword proceeded out of his mouth: and all the fowls were filled with their flesh." Revelation 19:20–21.*

Satan is captured, wrapped in a great chain and cast into the bottomless pit, which is then shut and sealed for the duration of Christ's reign on the earth—a thousand years, *"And I saw an angel come down from heaven, having the key of the bottomless pit and a great chain in his hand. And he laid hold on the dragon, that old serpent, which is the Devil, and Satan, and bound him a thousand years, And cast him into the bottomless pit, and shut him up, and set a seal upon him, that he should deceive the nations no more, till the thousand years*

***should be fulfilled: and after that he must be loosed a little season." Revelation 20:1–3.***

Jesus with the righteous will reign here on earth in absolute peace and righteousness for a thousand years. What a marvelous time. The Bible provides us beautiful insight to the thousand-year reign of Christ. There will be nothing that pollutes, nothing that harms, no wild animals, no war of any kind, no implements of war. What a marvelous period. Also, there will be no need for greedy, power hungry environmentalists. No infant deaths, and children will not be raised for trouble, states Isaiah 65:23.

Together we have studied, with the accuracy of the scriptures, the Antichrist, the False Prophet, the mark of the beast, idolatry, the tools they will need, and God's divine opposition to Antichrist. Hopefully we have allowed the Word of God to speak for itself.

The Word of God never leaves us in the dark. It always answers our questions. However, when carefully studied, with the help of the Holy Spirit, we discover that some of our former teachings and theology have been unsound. So what do we do? If we are smart, we drop our unsound theology and simply embrace the exactness of the Holy Scriptures.

We have learned that the Antichrist has a plan, is very capable and satanically anointed. He is assigned by Satan to try to accomplish what Satan himself cannot do: Conquer the earth and take it from our heavenly Father. Remember, Satan is our eternally DEFEATED FOE.

We have discovered the Antichrist has opposition from God through the 144,000, the two witnesses and angels through his seven-year tenure. He also has had opposition from within (Daniel 7:20) and destroys three nations that originally supported him. Opposition from without: the 200 million man Oriental army threaten him during the first 13 months of the Tribulation.

Daniel 11:44 reveals the westward movement of the Orientals and how it troubles the Antichrist. However, rather than do battle, they merge to resist the return of Jesus and His saintly army. He, the Antichrist, is completely and eternally finished. The 1,000-year reign of our Lord Jesus is found in Revelation 20. Satan is captured and released after 1,000 years. He must finally attempt to do what he has hoped others would accomplish for him, conquer the world. Revelation 20 reveals his release from the bottomless pit and final defeat. He then joins the Antichrist, false prophet and their followers forever in the lake of fire and brimstone.

I pray this book has edified you, encouraged and motivated you. Now you should be stripped of fear, built up in the things of God, and have better understanding. Do not allow speculation, sensationalism and misguided voices to deceive and mislead you, thereby opening the door of your soul to fear. II Timothy 1:7 states, ***"God has not given us a spirit of fear, but of power, of love, and of a sound mind."***

Believe the Word of God over all other voices and sources of information.

If you do not know Jesus as your personal Savior, from your innermost being, pray this prayer:

Lord Jesus, I recognize you as the Son of God whom God raised from the dead. I ask you to come into my heart. Wash me from all my sins with your blood that I might be acceptable to our Heavenly Father.

I now receive You and I want to know You as the Lord of my life. Thank you, Jesus. I am saved, born again and ready to begin spiritual growth as a child of God. Amen!

> ***"For God so loved the world, that he gave his only begotten Son, that whosoever believeth in him should not perish, but have everlasting life."***
>
> *—John 3:16*

> *"That if thou shalt confess with thy mouth the Lord Jesus, and shalt believe in thine heart that God hath raised him from the dead, thou shalt be saved. For with the heart man believeth unto righteousness; and with the mouth confession is made unto salvation."*
>
> *—Romans 10:9–10*

> *"Therefore if any man be in Christ, he is a new creature: old things are passed away; behold, all things are become new."*
>
> *—II Corinthians 5:17*

It is one thing to accept Jesus as one's Savior, but the next step is to become His disciple. In order for one to be discipled, he or she must find a pastor and a congregation of people who are led by the Holy Spirit to follow Jesus and serve Him.

Because of the fulfillment of Biblical prophecies, we know Jesus is coming soon.

> *"Therefore be ye also ready: for in such an hour as ye think not the Son of man cometh."*
>
> *—Matthew 24:44*

> *"Not forsaking the assembling of ourselves together, as the manner of some is; but exhorting one another: and so much the more, as ye see the day approaching."*
>
> *—Hebrews 10:25*

I rest my case, based only on the Holy Word of God.

## Evangelizing the World through the Prophecies of the Scripture

**Hilton Sutton** is regarded by many as one of the world's foremost authorities on Bible prophecy as related to current events and world affairs. Celebrating over fifty years of ministry, Dr. Hilton Sutton presents the prophecies of the scripture in an edifying manner, free from doom, gloom, and speculation. He dismisses commonly taught but unbiblical eschatological world government ruled by a world dictator, and a great falling away. Instead, he clearly demonstrates that the Bible foretells prosperity throughout the closing hours of this age, and the greatest harvest of souls ever by the glorious, victorious army of God, the Church; a harvest that, after the Rapture of the Church, will continue to grow throughout the seven years of Tribulation until we return with Jesus and all the saints to establish the first and only world government, the one thousand year reign of our Lord.

## OTHER BOOKS BY HILTON SUTTON TH.D.

*The Next Resurrection*

*Discovering Ancient Prophecies*

*The United States in Prophecy*

*Revelation Revealed*

*The Revelation Teaching Syllabus*

*Deacons*

## AUTHOR CONTACT

For more information regarding this ministry contact us at:

Hilton Sutton World Ministries
P.O. Box 1259
New Caney, TX 77357

Phone: (281) 689-1260
Fax: (281) 689-1265
email: hsm@hilton-sutton.org
www.hilton-sutton.org